サーギル博士と巡る
東大哲学散歩

— 場の地理学的解釈に向けて —

ジェームズ・サーギル　円光 門 著

編集協力：公益財団法人 東京大学新聞社

JN066324

シーズ・プランニング

目 次

目次

世界を想像する──地理的思考の重要性について──　1

写真撮影＝高橋祐貴（写真1、2）

円光　門（写真3〜19）

序論

世界を想像する

― 地理的思考の重要性について ―

ジェームズ・サーギル

（翻訳＝円光 門）

はじめに

本書はある種の実験であり、地理的解釈を通じて東京大学の象徴的な2つの空間である本郷キャンパスと駒場Iキャンパスを再構成し、再紹介する一連の空間的な問いかけである。

その目的は2つあり、第一の目的は、本書の読者の多くが熟知しているであろう、大学に属する様々な建物や空間を、一連の文化地理学的な分析と理論的な揺さぶりを通して提示することで、空間の見落とされがちな周縁的要素を明らかにすることである。ここでは特に、キャンパスの歴史、その建築形態、キャンパス空間の区分けと組織化、キャンパスを利用したり通過したりする個々人の動き、その他の様々な地理的特徴について言及している。

第二の目的は場が(たとえ大学のような「普通の」場であっても)時間、記憶、想像力の積み重ねによって生み出され、仕事、勉強、余暇などの理由でその場を行き交う人々がさまざまな形態で出会う方法を明らかにすることである。そのような場の物理的(物質的)、感情的、感覚的(非物質的)な構成や、そこでの体験を構成する根本的な要因については、一般的に知

2

られていない。そこで本書の読者が、日常生活の中で出会う場について、新たな見方、想像力、経験を見出してくれることを期待している。さらに、本書で提示された観念を、自分の住む場や空間の分析に応用し、自分の住む世界について「地理学的」に考え、人々が住み、働き、遊ぶ場を形成する社会的、文化的、歴史的な痕跡や存在を明らかにすることを、本書は読者自身に促している。

本書は、東京大学の学生新聞「東京大学新聞」に2年間（2019年〜2021年）にわたって毎月掲載された連載記事「サーギル博士と歩く東大キャンパス」を大幅に加筆修正したものである。これらの記事がこうして出版されたことは、連載記事を企画しただけでなく、私との何時間にも及ぶ議論を簡潔で魅力的な読み物に凝縮し、翻訳することに努めた円光門氏の功績によるものである。記事の核となる目的は、文化地理学の理論と方法論を空間の分析に応用することであるが、我々の議論と分析は、建築、歴史、文学、哲学、政治など、多くの分野に及んでいる。このように、議論の概念的基盤は、単一の読み物や方法論に限定されない、まさに学際的なものであり、さまざまな背景や関心を持つ幅広い読者の方々にアピ

ールできるものだと考えている。

　もう一つの重要なポイントは、本書の後半部分でオンライン空間、つまりバーチャルな地理の概念と経験を扱うという明らかな方向性の転換が行われていることである。インタビューの多くはキャンパス内で直接行われたが、新型コロナウイルスの発生と急速な蔓延により、キャンパス内で安全にインタビューを行うことができなくなった。つまり、このプロジェクトは実世界や、物理的な場に焦点を当てているのにも関わらず、大学のキャンパスが閉鎖され、移動や交流が制限されたことで、我々はこのプロジェクトに対するアプローチや、場や空間を議論する方法を再考することを迫られたのである。実際、世界中の大学において、教室の空間を再定義することが直ちに必要になった。それは物理的な大きさや照明、座席の配置などではなく、①何が学習の場としてふさわしいか、②それをバーチャルな環境でどのように実現するべきか、③学生やスタッフが遠隔での学習や仕事という「ニュー・ノーマル」をどのように体験するかという点にあった。文化地理学者の視点から見ると、二〇二〇年初頭にオンライン教育が急速に導入されたこと、空間を利用し体験する方法が再考されたこと、そしてオンラインで価値のある学習体験を構築するのに必要な技術が開発されたことは、

いずれも大きな関心事であり、地理について語るときの意味について考える上で有用である。

このように、本書に掲載されているエッセイの多くは、オンライン環境における距離、存在、不在の問題と、それらが物理的な世界にいる我々に与える影響を特に取り上げていることを目的としていることに、読者は気づくだろう。これらは、記憶、物語、場、流動性といった、文化地理学者が関心を寄せるさまざまな空間形態を読み解くための主要な要素となるテーマを中心に展開されている。これらの概念は、インタビュー全体に織り込まれており、読者に文化的、地理学的探求の主要なテーマについての洞察を与えている。

先に述べたように、このインタビュー形式のエッセイ集は、東京大学の2つの有名なキャンパス、本郷と駒場Ｉの場と空間、そしてその主要な特徴を、文化地理学のレンズを通して分析することを試みるものである。多くの読者にとって「地理」という言葉は、物理的な地理、つまり我々を取り巻く環境の一部として存在する山、川、砂漠、耕地などの地形を研究する学問として解釈されるであろう。また、ある人にとっては「地理」という言葉は、地形のマッピングや調査、人口増加や人口動態の変化、地政学的な境界線を追跡することだと思

うかもしれない。また、「地理」とは自治体の計画、農村と都市の区分、地名、貿易ルート、領土、紛争などのイメージにもつながるであろう。だが実際には、地理学はこれらの全てであり、そしてそれ以上のものでもある。

物理的な意味での地理（地形の研究）と人文学的な意味での地理（人や場の研究）には確かに区別がある一方で、地理そのものは全ての存在と密接に結びついている。即ち、地理は全てに関係しており、全ては地理的な観点から考えることができるということである。これは、地理学が正確性や一貫性に欠けた学問であるということではない。それどころか、地理学は、特定のものの間に存在する近接性、距離、移動、相互作用、越境などといった多数の空間的関係と、これらの関係が生み出す特定の空間的コンテクストを研究する学問なのである。地理学者が「全ては地理である」と言うとき、それは対象の重要性を示す根拠のない主張でもなければ、大雑把な一般論でもなく、むしろ、全てのものが時間と空間の両方に設定された客体として存在する方法を示しているのである。地理学者が特に関心を持っているのは空間的な次元であり、彼らはこの次元に焦点を当てて研究を行っている。

「地理」（Geography）という言葉は、古代ギリシャ語の geographia に由来し、それは簡単

6

に言えば「地球の記述」や「地球の説明」を意味している。つまり、地理学とは、その最も純粋な形において、我々の住む世界を描写する方法であり、場、空間、人々とその環境との関係を、生活と想像の両面から研究する学問なのである。したがって地理学者は、地球の物質的特性と、その表面に分布されている人間の社会や文化の両方を調査している。もちろん、すべての地理学者が地理の同じ側面に関心を持っているわけではなく、この学問分野にはいくつかの細分化された分野（文化地理学、歴史地理学、文学地理学、政治地理学など）が存在している。

時間と空間

文化地理学とは、文化が生み出される場や空間、景観を研究する学問であり、本書の中核となる考え方や方法論の多くがこの学問分野から引用されている。地理学者のジョン・アンダーソンは、「文化」とは人間の活動のすべての側面を表しており、物事が起こる場としての地理は、その活動に文脈を与えるものであると述べている（Anderson 2010）。このことは、我々が日常生活で行うことは、それを行う場や空間を通じて、（一つであれ、複数であ

れ）特定の意味を持つようになるということを示唆している。我々は、歴史上の出来事について、このように考えており、ある出来事、観念、紛争などが、その特別な時間の枠の中で発生したからこそ起こったのだとしばしば想像する。例えば、かつて人々は地球が平らだと信じていたが、このよく知られた誤解は、世界地理の歴史的理解の文脈を提供するため、即ち特定の時期に人々は世界のあり方について特定の信仰、または空想を抱いており、その地点から我々は進歩したのだということを示すためにしばしば言及されている。そう言及することで我々は、あらゆる歴史的瞬間にはそれが起こった時代の結果としての文脈が与えられている（あるいは、少なくとも文脈を得ていると想像されている）ことを明確に示しているのである。その文脈が科学技術の限界によるものであろうと、社会構造や宗教的信念によるものであろうと、大差はない。重要なのは、時間が、より一般的には歴史が、なぜ物事がそのように起こるのかを理解する際の決定要因であると考えられていることである。

しかし、もちろん、時間はすべての物事が作用する次元のひとつにすぎない。地理学者は、空間が思想、政治、信念、習慣、出来事など、（現在と過去両方において）我々の日常生活を形成するために行われているあらゆることに文脈を提供する（一つまたは複数の）方法に焦点

を当てている。地理学者ドリーン・マッシーはその代表作『空間のために』（2005年、原題：For Space）でまさにこの次元の重要性を強調した。マッシーによれば、空間とは分子レベルから地球規模に至るまでの継続的な相互関係の産物であり、どのような方法で定義するにしても、空間は異質であり、複数であり、常に生産の過程にある（Massey 2005: 9）。この空間的次元をよりよく理解し、それが我々の存在にどのように影響するかを知るために、さまざまなアプローチがとられてきた。例えば、日本の思想家である和辻哲郎は、哲学書『風土』（1935年）で、気候と文化の密接な関係、さらには空間性を存在の重要な側面として認識することの重要性に焦点を当てた。和辻の気候に関する研究は、ドイツの哲学者マルティン・ハイデガーの時間への執着に対する批判でもあった。ハイデガーの著作は、ニーチェやキルケゴールといった西洋の主要人物の著作と並んで、和辻の哲学的発展にとって特に重要なものであり、『風土』はこのドイツ人思想家の著作へのオマージュであると同時に批判でもある。ハイデガーは自らの存在論的分析において場にはほとんど注意を払っていなかったものの、ハイデガーの著作における空間と場、つまり地理学の役割は、地理学者や哲学者にとって持続的なインスピレーションの源となった。特にハイデガーの「住居」という概

念は、場の越境的な性質についての多くの研究を促した。「住居とは、環境や場を取り込みつつ、それを超えて広がっていくものであり、我々が現在の世界へと不可避的に浸っていることを意味すると同時に、新たな場、経験、観念に到達する可能性があることをも意味するものである」(Seamon and Mugerauer, 1985, p.8)。

ハイデガーと空間性を語る上で、オーストラリアの哲学者、ジェフ・マルパスの存在を抜きにしては語れない。マルパスはその生涯を通じて、ハイデガー的な空間性の調査に取り組んできた。空間性とは、本質的には、すべてのものは成長し続けるトポロジーの中に存在するというハイデガーの推測を前提としたものであり、そのトポロジーとは、存在が周囲の世界に近いか、あるいはつながっているかでしか測れないものだとされている(Malpas, 2008, p. 76)。マルパスはハイデガーの存在論における場の重要性を主張し、人間と非人間が互いに関係する仲介役として理解するための導線として、時間的にも空間的にも自然なプロセスである「住居」の役割を明らかにしている(Malpas, 2008)。ティム・クレスウェルが評しているように、ハイデガーにとって「住居としての場は、人間界と自然界を結びつける精神的・哲学的な試みである」(2004, p.22)。本論に続くインタビューで明らかにされることであ

10

歴史的、地理的な手がかりを探すいわば「場の探偵」（place detective）の役割を果たさなけ

しようと思う。そのために私は、東大キャンパスの変遷と我々の関係性の背後にある物語のことで、場が今は隠されている側面の痕跡、断片、記憶を通して我々に姿を現す様を明らかにていることを理解するのに役立つ。本論に次ぐ一連の議論で私はこうした考え方を用いるこ我々の場に対する経験が隠蔽されたものであり、常に現在の形によって部分的に覆い隠されが完全に把握することができないものの世界のことである。このような空間認識の解釈は、満ちた地理を提示している。「射映」とはつまり、不在の存在と存在の不在、すなわち我々が落とす多くの影」（Engelland 2020）である。この目的のために、ハイデガーは「射映」に象学の研究で言及した「射映」の発展形であり、「我々によって探求されるときに、物体自体ることができない（Heidegger 2003）。これは、ハイデガーの師エドムンド・フッサールが現に対して開示されている状態にある一方で、我々は観察したものの一部、一面を一度しか見ハイデガーにとって、世界は開示と隠蔽の場であり、人、物、道具などの物事は常に我々は彼の哲学が我々に与えてくれる空間的な両義性によるものなのである。るが、ハイデガーの著作は、地理学者としての私の仕事にも大きな影響を与えており、それ

11

ればならない。

場

地理学的探究の根本には場の概念、つまり我々が特定の場に愛着を持ち、そこでの経験に意味を見出すことを可能にするものが存在する。場は、地理学の他のどの概念よりも、我々が自分自身を世界に固定する方法において核心的位置を占めるものであると私は主張する。場は想像されるだけでなく、記憶される。我々の記憶は、我々の身体と同様に、他のすべてのものと同じ2つの次元、すなわち時間的次元と空間的次元に支配されている。12世紀の神学者アルベルトゥス・マグナスは、何かを思い出すときには、まずその記憶を場に固定することなしには考えられないと主張した(Carruthers 1990)。では、特定の場と結びつかない記憶は、どのようにして定位すればよいのだろうか。全ての経験が「場」と「時間」の両方の次元において起こるのであれば、空間的な要素を、想起される時間的な要素から切り離すことができるだろうか。各々が持つ最もはじめの記憶を思い返してみれば分かる通り、我々はその都度の人物や感情についてのみならず、それが現れた場についての認識をも、正確で

あれ不正確であれ、心の内に留めている。私が10代のときに亡くなった祖父のことを考えるとき、私は祖父のお気に入りの椅子、工具小屋、祖父母の庭などといった「場」においてまさに存在する祖父のことを思い浮かべる。祖父は、空間的な文脈を持たない不定形の人物、色、音として想起されるのではなく、記憶された地理的な集合の中に固定され、配置されているのである。

　人間は、場で考える。動物として、我々は場で考える。記憶した場に移動する動物、自分だけが思い出すことのできる場に隠れて冬眠する動物、特定の場で繁殖するために毎年移動する動物、自分だけが知っている特定の狩場で獲物を探す習慣のある動物など、複雑な思考プロセスを持つ全ての動物がそうであると考えることができるかもしれない。我々の世界も、彼ら動物たちと同じように、心の奥底に隠された複数の記憶された場の体験として展開されている。これらの場は、我々が身の回りの複数の複雑な空間を占有して生息する際に、保存され、想起され、回想される。つまり我々にとって、全ての場は新しいものではなく、空間的な経験は、少なくとも部分的には、多数の既存の記憶の結果であるのだ。それらは重ねられ、層を成し、高く積み上げられ、知らず知らずのうちに意識にのぼってきているのである。

言い換えればそれらは、我々が周囲の環境を理解するために恒常的に借用する「在庫品」なのである(Thurgill 2014, pp.85-86)。

想像的地理

我々が住み、移動する場、空間、景観は、それ自体が社会的関係によって形成されているという理解、これが文化地理学の重要な考え方である(Mitchell 2005)。つまり、我々の周囲に外的に存在する物理的な地形、つまり土、岩、水、空気などは人間の行動とは無関係に存在しているわけではない。歴史地理学者のフェリックス・ドライバーが指摘するように、地理とは、野原や山、川などの具体的な形で存在するだけでなく、我々自身の思考や周囲の人々の思考によって想像され、表現され、形成されるものである(Driver 2013)。ドライバーは「想像的地理」という言葉を使い、世界についての我々の考えが、抽象化、異国化、疎外のプロセスを通じて形成されることを説明した。19世紀のイギリスの地図(とその製作者)を例に、帝国主義的な思考が地理的な想像力に与える影響を示し、不当な社会的・人種的ヒエラルキーを実現するために、人々の地理的理解が歪められ、国民のアイデンティティ、人種的、社会

14

的発展、文化的価値に対する認識が操作されたことを証明したのである。

地理は場によって、また人によって異なるイメージを持たれていることを考える上で、地図は興味深い出発点となる。例えば、あなたがこの本を日本で読んでいるとしたら、日本を中心とした世界地図に慣れ親しんでいることであろう。つまり、日本は外の世界が立ち現れる中心点として固定され、そこからすべてのものが回転しているのである。例えば、イギリスで作成された世界地図と比較すると、日本に代わってイギリスが世界の中心、文化や経済の中心となっていることがわかる。このように、地理学は我々の物理的な世界とのつながりだけでなく、我々が世界をどのように想像し、それをどのように表現するかということにも関係しているのである。ここで重要なのは、「想像力は個人的なものであると同時に社会的なものである」(Driver 2013)ということと同時に、地図の中で、または地図によって表現されている地理的な想像は、その性質上共有されたものであるということだ。我々は他者を表現し、想像するという集団的なプロセスを通じて、異なる村、町、都市、地域、国の人々を、彼ら個人としてではなく、彼らが住む場、我々が住む場、そして我々の手による彼らの表象に基づいたステレオタイプとして見るようになるのである。

国内や地域内においても、地図やマッピングは同じような偏見で生産されることが多い。ポール・ファーリーとマイケル・シモンズ・ロバーツが書いているように、地図は常に抽象化のプロセスを経て生産される（Farley & Roberts 2012）。地図は決して客観的なものではなく、その中に何を含めるべきか、何を含めるべきではないかという決定が熟慮の上になされている。我々が住んでいる景観を視覚的に表現するものとして、地図は我々が自分の周囲の世界について理解し、道案内するためには不可欠なものだ。つまり地図製作者の偏見は、我々自身の偏見となる。マッピングは、実際にそこにあるものの記録であると同時に、地図から取り残されたものにも関係するのである。拙稿でも論じたように、地図から取り残されたものに着目することを通じて、我々は地図を創造的な道具として新たに利用することができる。つまり公式の地図では度外視されるような、未表象、未掲載の場を探索することで、「周囲の環境に対するより深くよりニュアンスのある理解を成立させるような意味ある経験を得る」ことが可能になるのである（Thurgill 2019, p. 9）。

「表象」は、社会的プロセス、包括的な政治構造、イデオロギーシステム（資本主義、共産主義、帝国主義、ナショナリズム、人種差別など）に応じて、地理がどのように想像され、解釈されるかを示す概念枠組みとして、20世紀後半に人文地理学者の注目を集めた（Anderson 2010）。ロラン・バルトやミシェル・フーコーといったポスト構造主義の思想家やフェルディナン・ド・ソシュールの記号論に影響を受けたこれらの表象文化地理学は、人々の世界に対する理解がどのように生み出されていくのか、そしてこれらの理解が、特定の地域、地方、国レベルで存在する記号や文化的コードの共有システムを通じてどのように意味を獲得していくのかということを検証、論証するために用いられている（Cosgrove and Jackson 1987; Jackson 1989）。文化地理学の現代的なアプローチは、地理というものがどのように現れ、経験され、生きられ、実行されるかということを考える際に、表象以外の方法論に焦点を当てることが多い。だが我々は、地理分析における表象の価値を見過ごしてはならないのである。

地理的想像力、つまり我々が自分の周囲の世界について考え、視覚化する方法は、もちろん地図製作者だけでなく、より一般的に文学、映画、テレビ、広告、政治、ニュース放送な

どの表現を通して、具体的には作家、監督、政治家、メディア企業によって我々に伝えられる言葉やイメージを通して形成される。全国紙を見るだけで、地理や地理的境界に対する我々の認識がどのように操作されているかがわかるであろう。どの国においても、政治的に最も保守的とされる新聞の紙面をめくれば、想像上の境界線が作られ、物理的な国境が強化されていることがすぐにわかる。例えば、イギリスの Daily Mail 誌は、移民、少数民族、LGBTQ+ コミュニティ、自分たちの政敵を特に否定的に描く記事を長年にわたって掲載しており、その結果、学者から多くの批判を受けてきた(Kundnani 2001; Gillborn 2010; Fox et al 2012 を見よ)。Daily Mail 誌が英国で最も読まれている新聞になったことを考えると(Wood 2020)、その政治的偏向報道や度重なる誤報の影響力を無視することはできないだろう。こうしたジャーナリズムは、暴力やテロリズムなどの反社会的行動を想起させる記事を通して、読者に自分とは異なる地理的ルーツ、民族、政治的スタンス、セクシュアリティ、宗教を持つ人々に対しますます否定的な考え方を形成させるような効果を、現実世界において持つのである。ここで、地理は空間的な「他者」を作り出すために用いられている。

こうした「他者」化のプロセスは、ホスト国とは異なる人種、民族、文化的背景を持つ人々

18

が、地理的に外的な場に本質的に根ざしており、自国の文化の外にいる人々とは相容れない者であること、つまりは「外国人」として認識された個人を実存的脅威として捉えるという物語を通じて生産されるのである。

国家、地域、地方の境界は、このような（誤った）表象によって絶えず我々の心の中で強化される。政治的なレトリックとメディアの偏向報道は、人々が地理について考える方法や、異なる地理的領域との関係を定める上で、常に相互作用するものであり、世界と諸国民に対して人々が持つビジョンを歪めるものである。その一例として、ドナルド・トランプ前大統領が新型コロナウイルスに関するテレビ演説で使用した言葉が挙げられる。前大統領の言葉の裏にある意図を、政治評論家たちは見逃すことはなかった。彼らによれば、「トランプが『コロナ』という言葉を線で消し『チャイニーズ』と言い換えた演説の台本がカメラマンによって撮影されたとき、彼の言葉遣いの計画性が明示されたのである」(Viala-Gaudefroy and Lindaman 2020)。トランプがウイルスを「チャイニーズ」、「武漢風邪 (Wuhan Flu)」、「カン・フル (Kung Flu)」と表記したことで、感染源である中国に対して非常に具体的な空間的パラメータが設定されたのである。

このような言葉は、ウイルスに関することだけでなく、より一般的に、西洋の民主主義の敵対者としての中国についての人々の考え方に影響を与えるようになった。新型コロナウイルスをめぐる政治的（または地政学的）な偏ったレトリックの結果、欧米に住む多くの人々の心の中では、中国と中国国民こそが真の脅威として想像されるようになった。中国の責任を「暴露」することを目的とした陰謀論の嵐がオンライン・フォーラムに押し寄せられているが、多くの場合、管理者はほとんど、あるいは全く介入していない。現在、ツイッターでは「Stop Asian Hate」という言葉がトレンドになっているが、トランプの反中国的な言動が、最近ではアトランタのスパでアジア系女性6人が殺害された事件にまで至った、現在アメリカを覆っている反アジア感情の種を撒いたと考えることだけでも十分である。私は、トランプ自身に殺人事件の責任があると言っているわけではない。なぜなら、ウイルスが発生して以来、人種差別や外国人排斥の言葉を口にした政治家はトランプだけではないからだ。しかしながらこれらの事件は、言葉には結果が伴うということを我々に強烈に思い起こさせるものとなった。もしあなたが特定の民族の人々を犠牲にしたり汚名を着せたりするような言葉を使ったり、地政学的な対立を永続させるために意図的に真実を弄んだり、故意に感染源と

民族性を混同させたりするのであれば、最後に銃の引き金を引くのも、やはりあなた自身かもしれないのである。

なぜ地理学は重要なのか

もちろん、我々が自分の周囲の世界を想像する方法に影響を与える表象は、これらだけではない。文学、美術、音楽、映画、演劇なども同様に、地理的な想像力を形成する役割を担っている。本やテレビ、映画のスクリーンから広がる世界、詩や絵画、ダンスで描かれる景観は、我々が心の中に描く地図に新たな印象を与える。地理的な表現に批判的になることも大切であるが、他者の想像力によって、別のレンズで世界を見ることができるようになることも考慮しなければならない。物語、映画、マンガ、ポップ音楽などは、それぞれが新しい世界像を生み出す役割を担っているため、それらも学術的な調査に値するプロセスである。我々が消費するメディア、芸術作品、歌、ビデオゲーム、本などが、現実と想像の両方の場──それはしばしば我々の場とは全く異なる場である──に対する理解をどのように形成し、決定するかは、地理的想像力を理解する上で非常に重要である。さらに、ジョン・アンダー

21

ソンの「場が文化の文脈を提供する」という主張（Anderson 2010）を受け入れるのであれば、地理の文化的描写の役割は、何を表現しているかだけでなく、誰が、どこで表現しているかによっても評価することができるのである。

地理は、文化がどのように表象されているかを理解するために重要であるだけでなく、その表象がどこで形成されているかということも重要である。例えば、スクリーン上の東京の描写は、その映画がどこで作られ、誰を対象としているかによって、東京がどのように見られているかを教えてくれる。ドキュメンタリーのような文化的なテクストが、どこでつくられたかということは、そのテクストが自国の観客からどのような文化的批評を受けたかということを見てみるだけでも、表象を理解し、意味を読み解き、特定の場がどのように想像されているかを評価する上で重要なものであることが分かるだろう。例えば、西洋人の手による東京の描写は、混沌としたネオンや常に混雑している通りなど、ハイパーモダンで未来的な要素に焦点を当てていることが多く、19世紀に始まったエキゾチックでミステリアスな別世界としての日本の表現を引き継いでいる。しかし、日本映画で東京が登場するときは、はるかにニュートラルな都市設定であることが多く、人々が生活し、仕事をし、遊んでいる普通のあ

りふれた空間である。こうした表現上の差異は、単に東西の分離を意味するのではなく、世界のあらゆる国、地域、地方レベルで存在するものであり、表象する側とされる側の認識、経験、想像力の溝を浮き彫りにしている。

地理学というものは一見するよりもはるかに複雑なものである。文化地理学者は、地理を人間同士の交流や接触などあらゆる活動によって生み出されるものだと捉えることで、場、空間、景観の過去、現在、未来についての想像を再構成する。そして何よりも重要なこととして、文化地理学者は人と場の相互関係を強調し、物理的にも想像された世界においても、場が人によってつくり出され、人が場によってつくり出されるさまざまな様態を明らかにするのである。

サーギル博士と巡る東大哲学散歩

サーギル博士と巡る 東大哲学散歩①

本郷キャンパス　赤門

門が作る「不在」と「摩擦」

「なぜ有る物があって、むしろ無ではないのか?」これは、見えないものは「不在」であるとした哲学者ハイデガーの言葉だ。赤門周辺の空間を考える上で興味深いこととして、サーギル博士は赤門の出入り口における「空間の不在」に注目する。東大キャンパスの他の門とは違って、赤門は上に屋根を構え左右を重厚な塀に囲まれている。よって赤門前に立って東大構内をのぞく時、門の枠や塀で覆い隠されている向こう側の世界を見ることはできず、

それらは我々にとっては不在であるといえる。しかし門をくぐり抜けるという行為を通じて世界は我々の眼前で展開し、不在は転じて存在になるのだ。

「不在は存在を通じて認識され、逆もまたしかりです」とサーギル博士は語る。言い換えれば、赤門に覆い隠され「不在」となっている空間を把握することで、赤門からのぞくことのできる東大構内の風景があくまで全体の一部であることが理解され得るのである。こうした「空間の不在」への理解が、まだ見えぬものを見ようとする我々を門の中へと誘い入れる。

赤門は人々を招き入れるが、同時に人々を制限するというパラドックスを抱いているとサーギル博士は指摘する。文化地理学者ティム・クレスウェルは渋滞や空港の出国ゲートといった人々の移動を阻害するものを「摩擦」と呼んだが、サーギル博士によると赤門もまさに入ろうとする人々の動きに制限という「摩擦」を生じさせる(写真1)。

赤門には一つの大扉と二つの小扉があるが、開いている扉によって、人々の視界や動作は異なる。というのも、門という枠組みを通じてしか、人々は向こう側の風景を見られないのであり、向こう側に行くことができないからだ。ハイデガーは「ゲシュテル(枠組み)」という言葉を使って、存在の在り方が環境によって規定されていることを説明した。赤門が持つ

28

構造は人々の身体の動きを制限し、規定するゲシュテルなのである。

さらにサーギル博士は人類学者ヴィクター・ターナーが提唱した「リミナリティー」という概念を引用する。これは越境的な変化を指す概念で、ターナーは、神社や教会といった人間がそこに踏み込めば日常から脱却する変化を経験する場をリミナルな場とした。サーギル博士は大学もまた、俗世間から離れ学術に従事するという点でリミナルな場であると考える。赤門はまさにそのような二つの場の境界線として機能しているのだ。

◇

二つの異なる領域の間には、物質的でないにしろ何らかの壁がある。別の領域に入るためには門が必要だ。しかし、気を付けなければならない。確かに門は「空間の不在」を形成することで人々を中へと招き入れる働きを持つが、まさにその形成された不在によって人々の動きに「摩擦」を生じさせる。

グローバル化が進む現代社会での身近な壁の例として、異文化を思い浮かべる人もいるだ

写真1　赤門は「不在」を作ると同時に、人々の動きに「摩擦」
を与える

ろう。それはトランプ前大統領が提唱するような現実の壁でも、誰もが心の内に持つ壁でもある。

一般的に、異文化間には壁ではなく門を設置することが交流の第一歩だろう。だが安易に異文化交流をうたった結果、交流相手はあくまで非日常的な「リミナルな場」を提供し我々を楽しませてくれる人たちという認識を広めることにはならないか。あるいは、実際に門に入ろうとすると摩擦が生じ、逆に壁がより強調されることにはならないか。異質な者同士の交流において、壁と門という枠組みから離れた先に何を見据えるべきか、赤門を見ながら考えてみてもよいかもしれない。

サーギル博士と巡る 東大哲学散歩②

本郷キャンパス　三四郎池

人工と自然の絶え間ない闘争

水質汚染や温暖化に見られるように、我々人間は自然に対して環境破壊という「暴力」を働いている。三四郎池（写真2）は、そのような我々と自然の間の支配—被支配の関係性を見直す契機を与えてくれるとサーギル博士は言う。例えば池周辺に位置する岩々は、来訪者の足場を不安定にして、人間の思い通りにならない自然の存在を明らかにする。さらに、人間と自然の距離の近さも注目に値するものだ。「三四郎池の美しい自然を目の前にして、我々は

写真2　三四郎池に訪れた人たちに話し掛けてみると「自然がきれいでリラックスできる」という声が多かった

自然を利用する対象として捉えるのではなく、自然そのものの在り方を尊重し、それに親しみを覚えるようになるのです」

だが、これは本当の自然だろうかとサーギル博士は問いかける。「地理学者ドン・ミッチェルは、一見自然のように見える多くの風景も実は人の手によってつくられた『表象』にすぎないという、批判地理学（critical geography）的な考え方を提唱しました」。三四郎池の自然はあたかも昔から存在しているかのような印象を我々に与える。だが実際は草木、岩、滝、池に住む魚や亀、鳥の鳴き声といった典型的な「自然」の要素が、まるで美術館のように人工的に配置されているのだ。

さらに興味深いことは、我々と自然の非暴力的な関係性の構築を促してくれるこのような表象が、そもそも我々が自然に対して働いた暴力を通じて形成されているということだ。三四郎池の美しい環境を維持すること、すなわち池の水を入れ替えたり、雑草を刈ったりと定期的な手入れをすることは、ある意味自然に暴力を働くことである。「あらゆる『維持』は、一定の『暴力』を必要とします」とサーギル博士は指摘する。池の水が汚くなったり雑草が生えることは、自然が人間によって奪われた自分の領地を取り戻そうとする表れなのだ。

三四郎池における人工と自然の関係は、哲学者ハイデガーの次のような議論によって上手く説明できる。ハイデガーは『芸術作品の根源』という書物で、芸術作品は「世界（Welt）」と「大地（Erde）」の緊張関係の中に生まれると主張した。作品が提示する「世界」は、作品を構成する物体、すなわち「大地」を切り開こうとするが、逆に「大地」は「世界」を覆い隠そうとする。

この議論を三四郎池に応用するとどうなるか。三四郎池という「作品」は、人工的に表象された自然すなわち「世界」と、その構成要素である真の自然すなわち「大地」の緊張関係の中に生まれている。表象としての自然は、真の自然を切り開くことで、言い換えれば自然に暴力を働くことで創り出され、維持されてきた。それに対して真の自然は、表象としての自然を覆い隠すことで、人の手によって奪われたものを取り戻そうとする。このように、我々が尊いと感じる三四郎池の美しさの背後には、人工と自然の絶え間ない闘争があるのだ。

それでは、我々が三四郎池において感じる自然への親しみは、意味のないものなのだろうか。暴力的な背景に支えられた暴力への反省は、空虚なものなのだろうか。そうではないとサーギル博士は言う。「現状がはらむ矛盾をしっかり意識した上で、良い部分は享受すべき

です。それが『批判的に考える』ということですから」。三四郎池の自然美を手放しで称賛するのでもなく、それを支える暴力に絶望的になるのでもない。暴力的な背景は認識しつつ、三四郎池が我々に与えてくれる自然への親近感を大事にすべきだろう。それが真の自然保護の精神へとつながっていく。

サーギル博士と巡る 東大哲学散歩 ③

駒場Ⅰキャンパス　1号館

人工と自然の絶え間ない闘争

「我々が普段見逃しているいろいろなモノの痕跡に着目すること、歴史はそのような『日常的な考古学』によって発見され得るのです」とサーギル博士は語る。1号館は正にその実践の場だ（写真3）。中庭へとつながる入口の上のアーチには、旧制第一高等学校の紋章が残されている（写真4）。さらに足元を見ると、そこには紋章を刻んだマンホールがある。建物内に入り廊下の窓から中庭を覗くと、災害や空襲などの非常事態を想定して造られたと思わ

写真3　1号館の両端には草木が生い茂る

写真4　アーチに残る旧制第一高等学校の校章

れる地下道へとつながる階段を目にすることができる。

　1号館は関東大震災から10年が経った1933年7月に建設された。そびえ立つ時計台、そして駒場キャンパスでは数少ないゴシック様式が見られるこの建物は、周囲にアナクロニスティックな雰囲気を与えている。第2次世界大戦中に学生たちが時計台に登って爆撃機を見張っていたという噂や渋谷まで続いていると言われる幻の地下道の話は、真偽のほどは分からないものの、1号館の異様さから生まれ、語り継がれている。

　だが、この異様さの源は何なのか。サーギル博士によると、それは過去が現存するモノによって

42

写真5 中庭へ至る道は閉ざされている

表象された際に起こる、時間軸の揺らぎによるものだ。「過去は現在においては不在ですが、その不在が過去の痕跡を示すモノによって明らかにされた時、現在に居残るわけです。まるでそこにいてはいけない幽霊のように、過去がその場に取りつくのです」

　1号館の不可解な雰囲気は、時間だけでなく空間においても見出すことができる。1号館の両端には草木が生い茂り、正面には大木が植えられているため、安田講堂などとは違い我々は離れた地点からこの建物の全体を視野に収めることができない。さらに、建物は中庭を囲むようにできているが、中庭を通り抜けることはできず、正門の反対側に移動するためには必ず1号館をぐるりと回

らなければいけない（写真5）。というのも、本来は憩いの場であるはずの中庭への入り口は鉄の柵で閉ざされているからだ。建物の全体を認識できないということ、建物の中心にたどり着けないということは、1号館の本質が常に覆われていて、捉え難いという印象を我々に与え得る。

建物内では、その捉え難さは一段と増す。入り口を入ると薄暗く細長い廊下に出るが、廊下は建物の四隅でそれぞれ折れ曲がっているので、どこに立っていても一度に見渡すことのできるのは、建物の四辺のうち一辺だけである。言い換えれば、我々が角を曲がる度に見えるものが変わるので、建物の全貌を一挙につかむことはできないのだ。

モノの痕跡から示される過去と、建物の配置によって限定される我々の視野。これら時間と空間における共通点は「常に何かが覆い隠されている」ことだとサーギル博士は指摘する。過去は現在においては不在として覆い隠され、モノの痕跡を通じてしか我々はそれに触れることができない。1号館という建物もまた、一度に全貌をつかむことを我々に許さない。あらゆる存在物は、完全な存在と完全な不在の間で揺れ動いている。「対象とは、多くの特性を示すと同時に隠す単位である」と哲学者グレアム・ハーマンが言ったように。

サーギル博士と巡る 東大哲学散歩 ④

本郷キャンパス　総合図書館

歴史とは痕跡の取捨選択

『歴史』とは痕跡を選択し、提示することであり、これらの痕跡が積み重なって層を成してできるのが『場』なのです」。サーギル博士の言う「歴史」と「場」の関係性は、総合図書館周辺の空間に顕著に表れている。

総合図書館（写真6）は、1877年の東京大学の創設と共に旧図書館として建てられた。関東大震災の火災で焼失した後、1928年に再建され、現在に至るまで幾度か改修工事を

45

写真6　2015年から改修工事を行っている総合図書館

経験している。1986年に図書館前広場の改修を任された工学部の大谷幸夫教授（当時）は、自分が東京帝国大学在学中に戦没した同輩や後輩への追悼の意を込めて、広場の地面に曼荼羅のモザイク画を施した。

だが2015年から始まった地下書庫の建設を伴う改修工事により、曼荼羅のモザイク画は失われることに。他方、工事の過程で旧図書館の土台と加賀藩邸時代の水路石が発見された。土台は噴水周辺のベンチとして加工、再利用され（写真7）、水路石は石の表面が切り取られ、広場の同じ位置にはめ込まれた（写真8）。

このように総合図書館周辺の空間には複数の異なる時代の痕跡が存在するが、ある層の痕跡は保存され、別の層の痕跡は排除される。一部の痕跡が選択、提示されることが「歴史の語り」を形成するのだ。

江戸時代の水路石、明治時代の旧図書館の土台、そして戦争の記憶である曼荼羅。なぜ前者二つは保存され、後者は排除されたのであろうか。サーギル博士によると、痕跡がその場に根差しているか否かという「正統性」が理由の一つとして論じられ得る。「水路石も旧図書館の土台も、元からその場にありましたが、曼荼羅は後から恣意的に添えられました。従

48

写真7　ベンチになった旧図書館の土台

写真8　加賀藩邸時代の水路石

って、曼荼羅は保存にふさわしいほど『正統』ではないと判断されたのかもしれません」

だが、このような「正統性」の議論は短絡的だとサーギル博士は言う。「水路石にしろ土台にしろ曼荼羅にしろ、全てある時点で人の手によって恣意的に作られたものです。古いから新しいかという相対的な違いしかありません」

もう一つの理由として考えられるのは、戦争という極めて政治的なものに関わる記憶を排除することで図書館前広場を非政治的、中立的な場にしようとする意図の存在だ。「近隣住人が犬を散歩させ、家族連れが談笑し、学生が学問や将来について語り合う場であるこの広場が政治色に染まってはいけないと考えられているのかもしれません」とサーギル博士は指摘する。

だが、政治的でない場など存在するのだろうか。あらゆる痕跡は、今は存在しない時間や空間に関わるものであるから、ある種の記憶に他ならない。故に水路石や旧図書館の土台といった過去の痕跡も、言い換えれば記憶である。アイルランドの地理学者カレン・ティルは、記憶の場は「行為」と「政治」の相互作用の中に生まれると主張した。公の場に記憶が保存され得るのは、人々が定期的にその場に来て出来事を想起するという「行為」があるからで

50

あり、また特定の権力が、継承するにふさわしく、正確で正当な記憶とはどれかということ
を規定する「政治」があるからである。そしてこの記憶の規定に際し、さまざまな意志を持
つ権力者同士の力関係が作用する。「故に、一見政治とは関係ないように思える水路石や旧
図書館の土台も、図書館前広場に置かれることでその場を政治化しているのです」

そもそも、場から政治性を排除しようとすること自体が政治的だ。「本来曼荼羅は戦没者
の純粋な追悼を目的として設計されたものです」とサーギル博士は語る。「にもかかわらず、
寛容で先進的であるべき大学という場において、帝国や排他主義を喚起する戦争のイメージ
はふさわしくないと判断された可能性もあります」。そしてこのような判断は政治的な判断
に他ならないのだ。

空間が残す戦争の記憶

それでは、戦争の記憶は大学から完全に排除されてしまったのだろうか。サーギル博士に
よると、以下二つの理由により、それは否定されるだろう。

写真9　ところどころ見受けられるアール・デコ様式

　第一に、これまで我々は、図書館前広場をさまざまな時代の痕跡の層だと捉え、どの層が最も強く、どの層が最も弱いかを考えてきた。だが図書館前広場はこのように痕跡を階層的に示す側面だけでなく、水平に示す側面をも持つ。

　総合図書館は「内田ゴシック」と呼ばれるゴシック様式で建てられたことは有名だが、実はゴシック様式の中にアール・デコ様式が混在するとサーギル博士は指摘する。「屋根のシルエットや窓の配置に着目すると、直線をベースにした要素の反復を特徴とするアール・デコ様式が表れていることが分かります（写真9）。すなわち中世の様式であるゴシックと二〇世紀の様式であるアール・デコはどちらがどちらを覆

52

い隠すのでもなく、水平に並んで共存しているのだ。

さらに、総合図書館は他四つの機関と共に一つの建物を構成しているが、その内の史料編纂所は現在の総合図書館の再建と同じ1928年に建設され、新聞研究所（当時）、社会科学研究所、教育学部の建物はそれぞれ53年、54年、55年に建設されている。戦前と戦後に貼られた色の濃さが異なる新旧のタイルが、同じ建物の外壁に並んで共存しているのだ。以上のように、「縦の層」ではなく「横の共存」という文脈で図書館前広場を再解釈すると、一旦は排除された層である戦争の記憶も、さまざまな時代が共存する場に舞い戻らざるを得なくなる。

第二に、サーギル博士によると、場とはパリンプセストに他ならない。パリンプセストは、すでに書かれていた文字が消された上で新たな文字が書き加えられた古文書のことだ。一旦消された文字は、肉眼では判読できずとも痕跡は必ず残る。

イギリスの人類学者ティム・インゴルドは、痕跡を「付け加えられたもの」と「取り除かれたもの」という2種類に分けた。すなわち、痕跡は「それがある」という指標にも「それがない」という指標にもなり得るのだ。水路石や旧図書館の土台が広場に付け加えられたこ

写真10　かつてこの手すりの下にモザイク画があった

とで過去を示す痕跡として機能していることに疑問はないだろう。だが曼荼羅が広場から取り除かれたこともまた、れっきとした痕跡だと考えてほしい。戦争の記憶は、今もここに留まり続けているのだ。

◇

　元東京大学キャンパス計画室員で文化資源学が専門の木下直之名誉教授によると、曼荼羅は元々「広場の曼荼羅」という題名で大谷教授が考案した図書館前広場全体のデザインであり、モザイク画は失われても痕跡は存在するという。

　例えば、写真10の床の模様や手前の手すりは大

谷教授による設計だが、残り3面の手すりは改修工事の設計の責任者である川添善行准教授（生産技術研究所）により変更されたため、前者を「痕跡」と捉えることができる。

なぜ東大は戦争の記憶を留める努力をしなかったのか。「敗戦時に全否定したからだという他ありません」と木下名誉教授は考える。終戦五十周年に東大内で学徒出陣に光を当てた調査が行われたことがあったが、対象はあくまで学徒出陣に絞られ、それ以前の日清日露戦争にまでさかのぼって検証する企てはなかった。「『忘却』のひとことに尽きるのかと思います」

駒場Ⅰキャンパス　駒場池

迷信がもたらす意味

「存在することは知っているが、実際行ったことはない」。駒場池（通称「一二郎池」）について聞かれ、そう答える東大生は多いだろう。取材のため、駒場Ⅰキャンパスの隅に位置する池の周りにサーギル博士と１時間以上いたが、その間に訪れてくる人は１人もいなかった。

そもそも駒場池は「受験生が訪れたら浪人し、在学生が訪れたら留年する」という言い伝

56

写真11　立ち入り禁止区域のチェーン

えがあるように、あまり良い印象を持たれて
いない。サーギル博士がこれまで前期課程の
学生に向けて開講してきた文化地理学の授業
でキャンパス内の場を素材に怪談を書かせる
課題を出すと、多くの受講生は駒場池を舞台
に選んだそうだ。池から伸びる手が近くにい
る学生を引きずり込み、溺死させる、といっ
たように。

なぜ駒場池は気味悪く人を寄せ付けない場
になっているのか。立ち入り可能な区域より
も立ち入り禁止区域の方が広く設定され、池
の周辺にはそれらを示すチェーンが随所に配
置されていることは明らかだ（写真11）。だが
なぜ我々の進入が拒否されているかについて

写真12　遊歩道沿いの木が全景を見渡すことを阻む

は理由が全く明らかにされていないことが、この場の薄気味悪さに一役買っている。それを裏付けるように、池周辺の遊歩道に沿って生える木が駒場池の全景を見渡すことを阻んでいる（写真12）。この場所を完全に理解することを、我々は許されていないのだ。

「一般的な説明では、このような池の地理的状況を訪問者が知覚することで不気味さを感じ、それが浪人や留年にまつわる奇妙な言い伝えを形成していったのだと結論付けられるでしょう」とサーギル博士。「しかし私は、逆もまたあり得るのだと思います」。それはすなわち、ある場に関する言い伝えや先入見を基に、訪問者の知覚経験が形作られる可能

性である。

幽霊の迷信が人々に与える影響力を考えてみよう。「幽霊の存在は信じていないと言う人たちも、墓地で一晩過ごすことを想像すると怖がります。幽霊を見たり感じたりすることはないと思っているのに、彼らは一体何を怖がっているのでしょう？」とサーギル博士は問い掛ける。この問いを解決するためには、人は対象そのものよりも、幽霊という対象と迷信の「結び付き」に重きを置くと仮定する必要がある。

では、なぜ「結び付き」はそれほど強固なものなのだろうか。哲学者イマヌエル・カントは主著『純粋理性批判』の中で、意味を得るということは、概念を対象へと関係付けることであると主張した。概念とは頭の中で思考されたものであり、対象とは自己の外部に存在するものである。何も経験せず自分だけで考えていることは「空虚」、ただ外の世界の情報を取り入れるだけでそれらが何であるか考えないことは「盲目」であると見なしたカントは、概念と対象の両者を結合させることで初めて意味が生じると考えた。

よって、人が対象そのものよりも、対象と迷信の「結び付き」を重視するのは、人がそこに意味を見出したいからなのではないか。

駒場池の奇妙な言い伝えから発する薄気味悪さと

59

いった「概念」が、池の地理的状況という「対象」と結び付いた時、知覚経験が意味を持って立ち現れる。

それはまた、駒場池が一つの場（place）として誕生した瞬間である。文化地理学者ティム・クレスウェルは次のように語った。「人が空間（space）の一部に意味を与え、何らかの方法で接触した時、それは場（place）となる」

都度立ち現れる「世界」

空間（space）が人によって接触され意味を与えられたときに、それは場（place）として生まれ変わると考えると、駒場池は空間としては一つかもしれないが、場としては少なくとも二つに分かれるといえる。

先ほど述べたように、駒場池には立ち入り許可区域と禁止区域が存在する。許可区域では人は実際に池の縁まで行くことができるので、空間へと身体的に接触することを通じてその空間を一つの場として認識することができる。

60

それに対して禁止区域においては、我々は池入口の階段を上がった先からその区域を見下ろすか、あるいは地図を見ることを通じてでないと空間に関与できない。見下ろすといっても、駒場池周辺には木々が生い茂っているため、全貌を把握するには地図に頼ることしかできなくなる。だが「地図とは空間を観念化したものにすぎません」とサーギル博士が話すように、地図上では許可区域におけるような身体的な経験は不可能だ。結果的に両区域は場としては異なるものとなる。

この点は、ハイデガーの「世界」という概念から考えると、より一層明確になる。ハイデガーの主著『存在と時間』によれば、世界は初めから幾何学的空間として与えられているのではない。我々が身の回りのいろいろなものと出会い、その都度それらへの注意の向け方を変えていくことで、世界は毎回異なった形で現象するのだ。

例として池の両岸に架かった橋を考えよう。この橋は直線ではなく、2枚の板をずらしてつないだように真ん中で折れ曲がっている（写真13）。橋は細く両側に柵がないので、この橋を渡り始める際は踏み外さぬよう視線を足元に集中させねばならない。この瞬間我々が意識するのは、今まさに水の上を移動しているということであり、この水と私の関係性において

61

写真13　池に架かる橋

一つの世界が立ち現れる（この時運が良ければ向こう岸へと勢いよく泳ぐ蛇を目撃することができる）。

次に、橋に慣れてくると我々の視線は往々にして右側の風景に集中する。というのも、左方向には岩や雑草といったあまり見栄えのしない池の終わり（写真14）が存在するのに対し、右方向には形の良い木々に囲まれた奇麗な水面が広がっているからだ。ここにおいても世界が新たに立ち現れることになる。

だが橋の真ん中まで来ると、折れ曲がった方向に応じて我々の視線はいや応なしに左に向けられ、身体も向きを変えざるを得なくなる。その結果、池の終わりという世界が我々と出会う

写真14　池の終わり

ことになる。

　ハイデガーの世界概念から考えると、我々が許可区域の多様な現象と身体的に接触する際、その都度世界は異なった仕方で立ち現れるのであり、結果的に我々は実に多くの「場」と出会うことが分かる。そしてこのような「場」との出会い方は、階段を上がった先から見下ろしたり地図で位置関係を確認することしかできない禁止区域においては不可能なことだ。

　池の終わりを認識することは、駒場池を池として認識することにもつながるとサーギル博士は指摘する。駒場池は細長く途中でカーブがあるため、橋の上に立って右方向を見ると、池はあたかも延々と続く川の流れのように感じる。

63

だが左側にある池の終わりを目にすることで、我々は初めてこれは有限性、局所性を持った池であり、はるか先まで流れる川ではないことが分かるのである。サーギル博士は次のように語る。「池の終わりを見ることではじめて池そのものが分かるように、存在は不在があって初めて認識し得るのです」

駒場Ⅰキャンパス　数理科学研究棟

無機質性の背後にある有機性

駒場Ⅰキャンパスの端に位置する数理科学研究科棟（写真15）は、しばしば「数理病棟」と呼ばれる。確かに、コンクリートがむき出しの無機質な外観や簡素なエントランス（写真16）は「おしゃれに無頓着な数学科の学生」という固定観念と相まって、病院のような印象を与え得るのだろう。だが建物を普段とは異なる視点から見てみれば、別の世界が現れてくる。

「文化地理学の視点から考えて、この建物は東大キャンパス内で最も成功した建築物の一つ

写真 15　一見無機質な外観を持つ数理科学研究科棟

写真 16　簡素なエントランス

だと思います」とサーギル博士は言う。

そもそも文化地理学者に建物のことを語ることはできるのだろうかと疑問に思う人もいるだろう。構造物としての印象や機能性に関しては、もちろんその設計者である建築家が最もうまく語り得るものだ。だが、サーギル博士いわく「建物が空間にいかに適合し、あるいは空間をいかに創り出しているかを考えることは、文化地理学者の仕事でもあるのです」。

まず建物の中に足を踏み入れると、数理科学研究科棟は予想に反して「病棟」のように人の動きの効率性のみを重視する構造でないことが分かる。傾斜のある地形に沿った造りになっているため、1階と地下の境界線が曖昧になるような廊下があったり（写真17）、一部本館と連結している講堂が外にむき出しであったりするなど、あたかも迷路のような構造が我々に多元的な空間理解を迫るのだ。また、至る所で反復される三角や四角といった幾何学の形状は、簡素で硬直した建物の第一印象とは裏腹に、まるで生き生きとした数学の本質を描くようである。

「この建物は数学だけでなく周囲の環境とも強い関連性を持っています」とサーギル博士は語る。入り口前に広がる矢内原公園に着目しよう（写真18）。公園の向こう側に見えるガラ

写真 17　入り組んだ構造を持つ廊下

写真 18　研究科棟前の矢内原公園

ス張りの駒場図書館と比べれば、数理科学研究科棟は入る者を歓迎するような雰囲気を備えてはいない。だがその間に存在する円形の矢内原公園は、まさに「円形」という周囲のものを調和させる性質を通じて、二つの建物を緩やかに結び付ける。このように数理科学研究科棟はキャンパスの他の施設ともつながりを保っているのだ。

「一見無機質に思える緑や茶といった外観の色も、実は矢内原公園の木や土の色と重なり合っているのです」とサーギル博士は指摘する。この建物はあたかも周囲の自然に溶け込み、それと共存しているかのようだ。建物は人間の自然理解を構造物へと変換すると建築学者クリスチャン・ノルベルグ＝シュルツは述べたが、数理科学研究科棟はまさに周囲の自然と一体化することで、我々の自然理解を反映していると言えよう。

そもそも、数理科学研究科棟の無機質性はどこから来ているのだろうか。建物の外観は平たんな壁のようであり、キャンパスの限界を示す境界線を思わせる。このことが、建物が人けのないキャンパスの辺境にあることを際立たせているのだろう。だが窓が一定の角度を持って建物上部に斜めに配置され、空からの光がそれぞれの窓によって反射されていることに注目すれば（写真19）、空という無制限なものを反映した建物は、その途端自身も境界線から

写真 19　空を反射するガラス窓

超越した存在となる。

以上のように考えると、我々がこの建物に抱く印象も当初とは異なってくるのではないか。自然の一部としてこの建物を見なしたとき、それは味気ないコンクリートの塊などではなく、探究すべき「場」へと変貌するのだから。

サーギル博士と巡る 東大哲学散歩 ⑦

オンライン授業

オンライン授業は「場」の欠如か?

これまで取り上げてきた東大キャンパス内の「場」は、いずれも物理的に存在するものであった。だが新型コロナウイルスの発生直後、学生の入構は全面的に禁じられるようになる。この時期、我々に唯一残された東大にアクセスする方法はオンライン授業となった。状況はいずれ改善されるだろうが、本書執筆時点では、大学へのアクセスは制限されたままであり、授業の大半は引き続きオンラインで行われている。果たしてオンライン授業は文化地理学の

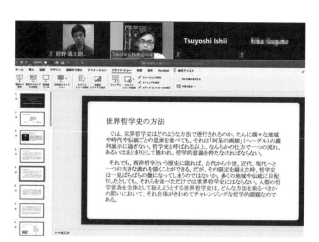

写真20　東京大学東アジア藝文書院が開講している講義の風景。Zoom を駆使して受講生の活発な発言を引き出している。

考察対象としての「場」となり得るのか。

「仮想世界における『場』の機能については、これまで多くの文化地理学者が論じてきました」とサーギル博士は話す。文化地理学者にとって「場」とは、人間が自身との関係性において「意味」を定位する所である。「『意味』は『場』が我々に喚起する感情や記憶などから生まれるのです」

よって授業中に教員や学生と交流することで思い出を作り、そこに自分なりの意味を付与することを可能とするオンライン授業もまた「場」と言うことができるだろう（写真20）。「場」はあたかも現実的な空間の中に存在するように感じられますが、それが現実である

か仮想であるかにかかわらず『場』の形成過程は常に各当事者の心の中にあります」

それでは、オンライン授業に見いだされ得る意味経験は、いかなるものだろうか。サーギル博士はハイデガーの「覆い隠し」という概念を軸に議論を展開する。「オンライン授業では、参加者の顔より下の身体が、カメラをオフにすれば顔が、そして表示名を偽名にすれば本名が認識不可能になります。普段の物理的な教室に存在するはずのさまざまなものが覆い隠され得るのです」

サーギル博士によると、このような「覆い隠し」は次の点で両義的だ。第一に、個々人の身体性が失われることで、参加者同士の自発的な交流が生まれづらくなる。だが同時に、顔や名前といった個別性が覆い隠されることは、参加者に何らかの連帯感を呼び起こすことがあるという。「どの学生も自分と同じ不便な状況下でパソコンのスクリーンを前に学習しているのだという連帯感です。つまり、普段教室で隣に座っているはずの学生がいないという

こと、この『不在』こそが逆説的に、私以外の人も『存在』するのだという共通認識を参加者全員に示すのです」

このように考えると、オンライン教室は物理的な教室とは違った良さを持っているように

思える。だが「そもそも現実と仮想という二項対立の思考法は、我々が物理的、外的な環境に依存し過ぎていることの象徴ではないでしょうか」とサーギル博士は問い掛ける。「私たちはこれまでコミュニケーションの場において、活動主体が物理的に現前する、すなわち『まさにここに存在する』ことを自明視、特権視してきましたが、最近ではこのような前提はオンライン学習の実践を通じて少しずつ脱構築されてきているのではないかと思います」

日常的な物理世界において我々を取り囲む言葉や図、風景、音楽、そして顔の表情といったものさえも全て、何らかの意味を表象するという点において記号であると言える。フランスの哲学者ジャック・デリダによれば、記号とは、それが指し示す当のものが不在である中、その現前性を代わりに表すものだ。すなわち、日常的な物理世界にあるものは、あたかも我々の目の前に存在しているかのように思えるが、実態は真逆であり、それらは意味を指し示すものとしての媒介に過ぎないことが多い。例えば、ある人物が私の目の前にいるからと

いって、私はその人物の存在を直接的に認識しているわけではない。喜怒哀楽を示す顔の表情、人種を示す肌の色、発言内容を示す言葉などの記号を介してのみ、その人物にたどり着いているのである。

74

よってオンライン授業と物理的な教室における授業との差異はそれほど大きくないことが分かる。オンライン授業において、我々は教員や学生の存在にパソコン画面に表示されている記号を介して間接的にしかたどり着けない。しかしこのような間接性の構造は、物理的な教室においても同様なのである。我々は必ずしも、現実対仮想という二分法にこだわらなくとも良いのかもしれない。

権力と空間

ここまではオンライン授業と対面の授業との共通点を探ったが、つぎに両者の差異に起因するオンライン授業の負の側面を取り上げる。そして、どのような発想の転換を通じてそうした負の側面を乗り越えることができるのかを考えてみたい。その際、考察対象を身体性の喪失と移動の制限という2点に絞ろうと思う。

第一に、オンライン授業で身体的な交流が少ないことは、対面の授業との差異を考える上で真っ先に思い浮かばれるものだろう。これは、オンライン授業において非言語的コミュニ

ケーションが成立しづらいことを含意する。というのも、相づちや表情、身体の向きといっ
た言語で明示的に表されることのない相手へのシグナルは、多くの場合身体から発生する。
従って身体性が喪失すれば、コミュニケーションも円滑に進まなくなる可能性がある。

これに対してサーギル博士は次のように応答する。「コミュニケーションが不十分になる
という問題は確かに否定し難いですが、身体性が喪失したからこそ生じた肯定的側面もある
のではないでしょうか」。サーギル博士いわく、そうした側面とは「場の民主化」だ。

「我々は普段、知らぬ間に権力関係を身体性の内に見いだしてしまっています」とサーギ
ル博士は語る。身体性がある、すなわち身体が空間に存在するとは、身体が位置を持つとい
うことであるが、位置関係とは多くの場合権力関係の転写である。「会議でリーダーがテー
ブルの短辺の方に座ること、授業で教員が黒板の前に立つことなどは、現実の権力関係を
表象、維持するものです」。だがオンライン授業では各参加者につき長方形の枠があるのみ
で、それは教員だろうが学生だろうが同じである。さらにカメラをオフにすると、存在する
のは個々人の声と考えるだけだ。「このようにコミュニケーションの経験が平準化されること
で、場が民主的になるといえるでしょう」

76

しかし民主政はそれ自体排除の論理と結び付いているという点に、注意が必要だ。西洋政治哲学の父プラトンの著作『プロタゴラス』では、神があらゆる人間に与えた正義に関する徳を訓練を通じて開花させれば、市民が自由な討論を通じて意思決定する民主政が成立するのだという議論が紹介される。だがその際、徳を十分に開花させられない者は民主政体に害を与えるとして死刑に処すべきだと論じられる。

このように、あらゆる人に平等な基盤を与える民主政は、その基盤に乗ることのできない人を排除してしまうという逆説的な働きを持つ。オンライン授業も同様であって、「声」と「考え」だけの平等な場だからこそ、例えば声を出すことのできない人は排除されることになる。だがこの問題は、オンライン授業特有の問題というよりは、民主主義や平等主義に内在する問題である。

これまで我々は身体性の喪失が権力関係を弱める点に注目してきた。だが他面で、まさにそれを可能とさせているオンラインシステムが、権力関係を強化する方向で働き得ることも忘れてはならない。

現在多くの大学が授業で採用しているウェブ会議システム「Zoom」では、ミーティン

グルームのホスト（大抵の場合は教員）に多くの権限が集中する。ホストは参加者のスピーカーやカメラをオフにする権限、参加者を別室へと移動させる権限などを持つが、このような教員と学生間の権力の非対称性は、対面の授業で見られるものではない。というのも、どれほど権力を持つ教員であっても学生を無理やり追い出したり、声を出させなくしたりすることとは、暴力に頼る以外に方法はないからだ。

この問題に対しては、サーギル博士は以下の通り応答する。「あらゆる場は人間が作らない限り存在しないというのが、地理学者の共通理解です。ミーティンググルームのシステムは、あくまでZoom社が作ったものにすぎないことを忘れてはいけません」

Zoomがもたらすコミュニケーションの枠組みを所与のものとして自明視すれば、ホストとその他の参加者の権力関係は固定されたものとして描き出されてしまう。権力関係を解体するには、それを構築する場そのものに疑いのまなざしを向けなければならない。

さらに広げて言えば、場がテクノロジーに媒介されていると自覚することの重要性はオンライン授業に限ったことではない。「感染防止策として、ビッグデータの活用などを通じて人の活動を統制することが本格的に論じられ始めている今、我々の日常生活を形成している

テクノロジーを当たり前のものとして捉えてしまうことは危険です」第二の考察対象である移動の制限の問題に移ろう。Twitter上で、オンライン授業はまるで牢獄で勉強しているようだという意見も見られるように、これは多くの学生を悩ませている問題だ。確かに我々は今、大学のキャンパス内を自由に歩いて教室へと向かうことはできない。オンライン授業への唯一の経路はURLをクリックすることで、教室間を移動する際に寄り道する楽しみもない。

サーギル博士はこの問題に対し「移動が制限されていることは現実の空間でも同じではないでしょうか」と問い掛ける。都市の面積の大部分は私有地であり、従って我々がアクセス権を持たない場がほとんどだ。店一つを見ても、客が入れる場とそうでない場は境界付けられている。にもかかわらず現実の空間においてあたかも移動の自由が存在するように思われるのは、我々が無意識に入れない場所をよけて都市を歩いているからにすぎない。

サーギル博士いわく「そもそも、場とは空間が制限され境界付けられることによって初めて生まれるのです」。現実の空間で意識されてこなかった「場」は、オンライン授業において先鋭的に現れる。

しかし他方で、我々は「時間」という重要な要素を見過ごしているのかもしれない。今回の結論はあくまで「空間」に着目したが故に導き出されたものだ。移動する間の「時間」が本質的なものだとしたら、我々はこの問題にどう向き合うべきか。引き続きサーギル博士と共に考えていきたい。

サーギル博士と巡る　東大哲学散歩 ⑧

オンライン空間

オンライン空間における時間経験

　前章において、我々は対面授業とオンライン授業の差異性をいかに乗り越えることができるかという問題に着目してきた。だが、そのような差異性を解消できていたのは、我々があくまで「空間」という要素を前提にして論じてきたからであって、もう一つの重要な要素である「時間」がこれまで見過ごされてきたことが、前章で明らかとなった。そこでこの章では「時間」を中心に、現実空間とオンライン空間の間には決定的な亀裂があるのかどうか、

検討したい。

『時間が存在する』と言うためには、全ての存在にとって根源的な次元である空間というものが措定されなければなりません」とサーギル博士は言う。カントは時間を、空間から独立した内的直観だと主張したが、実際のところ、空間なしに純粋な時間を経験することはできないだろう。我々は普段「日が沈んだ」「しばらく見ない間に髪が伸びた」「ずっと座っていたら腰が痛くなった」という形で、空間内のある存在における出来事を基に時間の経過を感じる。このように時間と空間は密接に関わり合っているが、現実空間とオンライン空間では、両者の関係はどのように異なるのだろうか。

第三章（駒場Iキャンパス1号館）や第四章（本郷キャンパス総合図書館）で述べたように、現実の空間においては過去のさまざまな時代の痕跡が層を成している。すなわち、一つの場所にとどまっていても、そこに位置するさまざまなモノを通じて過去を感じることができる。このように1カ所にとどまりながら現在と過去との行き来を示すものを「垂直的時間軸」と名付けよう。これに対して、ある地点から別の地点への移動を示すものを「水平的時間軸」とする。前者は「痕跡」に、後者は「移動」に関わると言ってもよい。

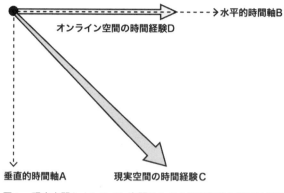

水平的時間軸B

オンライン空間の時間経験D

垂直的時間軸A　　　現実空間の時間経験C

図1　現実空間とオンライン空間における時間経験の差異は垂直的時間軸と水平的時間軸によって説明できる

　サーギル博士によれば、現実空間における時間経験は、常に「垂直的時間軸」と「水平的時間軸」という二重化のプロセスとして現れる。図1で示されている通り、AとBという二つの軸から、Cというベクトルが導き出される。すなわち、ある地点から別の地点へと移動する際、同時に私は現在から過去へとさかのぼり得る。私が一歩進むたびに、周囲の新たな痕跡に出会う可能性が生まれ、その場の時間的な「深み」が明るみに出るからである。

　しかしオンライン空間においては、様相が全く異なってくる。一つのウェブサイトという「場」から別のウェブサイトへと移動することがあるように、水平的時間軸はあると言えるだろう。だが

そこには過去の痕跡を示すモノが存在しないため、垂直的時間軸が欠けている。従って図1ではDというベクトルがオンライン空間上の時間経験を示すことになるのだが、Cのように2次元的な広がりを持たないため、極めて「平坦な」経験となってしまう。サーギル博士いわく、この時間経験こそが現実空間とオンライン空間を比較した際の決定的な差異である。

オンライン空間上の痕跡なき平坦な時間経験は、我々にどのような意味をもたらすのか。

「記憶の蓄積の場としてのアーカイブさえもがデジタル化されることで、〈いま〉が散逸していってしまうでしょう」とサーギル博士は分析する。だが、そもそも「〈いま〉が散逸する」とはどういうことなのか。

サーギル博士によると、我々が〈いま〉という感覚を持つのは、過去のアーカイブに関わることのできる限りにおいてである。「不在があってはじめて存在があるように、〈いま〉という意識は、過去との対比においてのみ現れるのです」。だがそれは、あくまでアーカイブが形を受けるという点で特定の媒体に依存するという点において有限性を持つ場合にのみ、当てはまるだろう。例えば、別れた恋人からもらったプレゼントは、かつて恋人と過ごした日々が保存されるアーカイブであり、石碑は遠い過去の重要な出来事を保存する記録である。

だが、プレゼントというという固有の媒体として、石碑は石碑という固有の媒体としてしか、我々に出会われることはない。このように、アーカイブはその存在の仕方が極めて限定されているというある種の「脆さ」を自ら提示することで、その出来事が「かつてあったが、今はもうない」という点を強調し、〈いま〉との対照性を際立たせるのである。

これに対して、オンライン空間においてはアーカイブはデジタル化されるため、そのような「脆さ」は消失する。オンライン講義は録画をして何回も繰り返し見ることができるし、クラウドにアップロードしたりUSBメモリに移管したりすれば、パソコンが壊れたらスマホで、スマホが壊れたらタブレットで見ることができる。現実空間で行動することに対する時間的拘束は仮想空間には適用されず、時間と空間の特異性はこのプロセスにおいて歪められるからだ。このようにデジタル化されたアーカイブは物理的な記録とは異なり、特定の媒体に依存することもなくなるので「かつてあった出来事」と〈いま〉の関係が異なってくるのであり、現実世界において我々が目撃する時間的な深さが失われていくのである。だが、このようにして仮想来事が反復可能となることで、〈いま〉は至る所に現れるのだ。過去の出来事が反復可能となることで、〈いま〉は現実世界の空間における〈いま〉ではない。サーギル博士はこの現象を

「〈いま〉の失敗」(the failure of now)と呼ぶ。

包括的排除と排除的包括

このように、現実空間とオンライン空間は、時間経験という点において、互いに和解不可能な亀裂を有している。だが、ここで注目すべきなのは、あらゆる区別や境界においては、正反対の方向性を持つ力が作動しているという点である。イタリアの哲学者ジョルジョ・アガンベンは、そのような場を「閾」(soglia)と呼んだ。

閾とは、二つの領域が互いを区別し合うと同時に交じり合う場である。これは一見逆説的に聞こえるが、アガンベンの主張は、あるものが他のものから自身を区別するとき、自身から他のものを排除しなければならない、ということである。アガンベンはこのことを政治と法の問題として論じており、特に例外状態は真に例外的なものではなく、究極的には通常状態を反映したものにすぎないという考え方を提唱している。つまり、例外的なものはすでに通常のものに包含されているのだ。このような包含の仕方には2通りがある（図2）。あるも

86

のが他のものを包含することでそれを排除する「包含的排除」（例えば、緊急事態の際に罰則を設けずに例外的な行為を可能にする法律上の例外条項）と、あるものが他のものの領域内に排他的な空間を占めることで、他のものをあるものから排除する「排他的包含」（例えば、実効支配されている領土）である。包含的排除と排除的包含によって、二つの領域の境界線は画定されると同時に曖昧になる。このような状況では、例外的なものと通常のものとを区別することは不可能になるのだ。

「ソーシャルディスタンス」という概念は、まさにそのような理由で境界線の両義性を表しているとサーギル博士は話す。授業や会議などはオンライン空間で行い、現実空間ではソーシャルディスタンスをとらなければならないという今日のライフスタイルは、現実空間とオンライン空間の境界線を我々により一層意識させるものであるが、サーギル博士は次のように指摘する。「ソーシャルという人と人との近さを示す言葉と、ディスタンスという隔たりを示す言葉を合体させて一つにすることは、矛盾を感じさせます。本来、隔たりがあってこのことは以下を意味する。現実空間がオンライン空間から区別されるのは、後者におい

は近づくことができないからです」

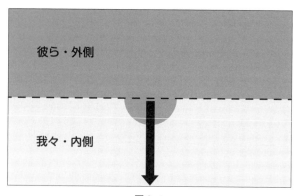

図2-1

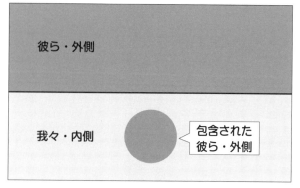

図2-2

図2 アガンベンによれば、我々・内側と彼ら・外側を区別する
ような境界線は、強固なものではない。
「包含的排除」においては、彼ら・外側の一部が我々・内側の領
域に包含されるため（図2-1）、その包含された彼ら・外側の部
分を否定することで、我々・内側と彼ら・外側との境界線を確立
することができる（図2-2）。

88

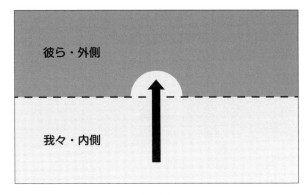

図2-3

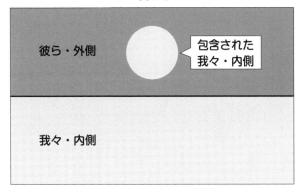

図2-4

「排他的包含」においては、我々・内側の一部が彼ら・外側の領域から排除されるため（図2-3）、その排除された我々・内側の部分を否定することで、我々・内側と彼ら・外側の境界線を確立することができる（図2-4）。

て経験される隔たりが前者へと持ち込まれ（包含的排除）、また前者において経験される人と人との近さが後者に持ち込まれる（排除的包含）ときである。例えば、現実空間で人と会う（「ソーシャル」の側面）ときにはマスクを着用しなければならないため、顔を見ることができない（「ディスタンス」の側面）が、オンライン空間で会議をする（「ディスタンス」の側面）ときなどは、当然マスクは着用しなくても良いため、顔を見ることができる（「ソーシャル」の側面）。サーギル博士いわく「私たちは近づくことで遠ざかり、遠ざかることで近づく。この矛盾を可能にしているのが『ソーシャルディスタンス』なのです」

以上に見てきたように、現実空間とオンライン空間の間には決定的な境界線があるが、それは両者が互いを区別し合うと同時に交じり合う場である。ウィズコロナの時代における我々は常にこの境界線に身を晒しているわけであるが、問題は、どのようにそれに向き合っていくべきかということだ。コロナ以前が良かったといって、対面にこだわるか、あるいは時代は変わった、今日の社会ではディスタンスは社会的であるために必要なものなのだと割り切って、オンラインで全てを済ますか。アガンベンは次のように述べる。同一の場に二つ

の相反する可能性が存在するとき、一方の可能性が他方の可能性に対抗して用いられるべきである、と。もはや従来の二者択一的な仕方で、現実空間とオンライン空間を解釈することはできない。我々は、新時代における時間認識と空間認識の転換を迫られている。

コロナ禍の世界空間

――新型コロナウイルスの感染拡大は決して医学の問題にとどまりません。欧米ではアジ
ア人が、中国ではアフリカ人が暴行を受けるなど、人種差別の問題にまで発展しています。
このことは文化地理学的な観点からはどのように論じられるでしょうか

　文化地理学における「文化」とは人間活動全般を指し、人間活動は常に何らかの空間の中
で展開します。人間がどのように特定の空間と結び付き、意味を見いだしていくのかを探究
する学問が文化地理学なのです。

　今回のパンデミックに付随して起きた外国人排斥感情を文化地理学的な観点から考察する
際に注目すべきことは、人々の空間認識が変容することで「他者」がどのように生じていっ
たかということです。新型コロナウイルスの発生が伝わり始めた頃は、世界中の人々、特に
欧米諸国の人々は、これはあくまで中国の問題だと認識していました。彼らにとって、欧米
と中国の間には想像上の空間的断絶があったのです。

94

──その後感染は欧米にも広がりました

　象徴的なのは、欧米諸国に住むさまざまなアジア系の人々が想像上の「アジア人である他者」という単一主体にまとめあげられることで、新たな空間化のプロセスが発生したことです。すなわち、ウイルスの感染範囲には空間的な制限があるという認識が崩れていったのと同時に、欧米在住のアジア系の人々が感染源だという誤った認識の下、空間的にもまさに間近にある脅威の対象として彼らが捉えられるようになってしまったのです。

──それでは次に、中国の側で起こったことを文化地理学的に考えるとすると、どのようなことが言えますか

　中国には、資本や金融を縦横無尽に移動させて世界各国と貿易を展開する経済的空間と、言論や情報を統制する政治的空間という二つの相反する空間が共存しているように見えます。

両者は、国内における権威主義的統治と国外におけるグローバルプレーヤーとしての振る舞いという矛盾の存在を象徴していると言えるでしょう。国内で新型コロナウイルスの発見に関する報告が当局によって抑圧されたというニュースは、中国が初期段階でウイルスを封じ込めることに失敗したことへの批判として、世界中のメディアで報道されました。

このようなウイルスに関する情報や言論の統制は、中国が国内向けの物語を作り出すことを目的としているかのように見えるかもしれません。しかし同時にそれは、世界市場における主要なトレーダーおよび製造業者としての国際的地位を維持するという国外に向けての動きと完全に切り離されているわけではないのです。グローバルプレーヤーとしての中国のアイデンティティーと権威主義としての中国の政治体制との間に不連続性があるように見えても、実は両者は本質的に関連しています。

ハイデガーの表現を借りれば、特に今回のパンデミックに関する情報の内部的 および外部的抑制は、真実を「覆い隠す」（verbergen）方向に働くことで、中国という国が境界の内側と外側双方から認識される仕方に影響を与えています。当局は報道機関を統制することで、貿易相手の喪失や工場の稼働停止といったパンデミックがもたらす経済的な影響を防止しよ

——ハイデガーは「覆い隠す」（verbergen）と「あらわにする」（entdecken）という二つの言葉をコインの裏表のような意味を持つものとして扱いますが、中国にもそのような両義性が認められるということでしょうか

中国の内と外の物語における空間の「覆い隠し」のプロセスは、閉鎖的な国家としての中国とグローバルパワーとしての中国の空間領域の差異を曖昧にしていますが、同時にそれは中国固有の在り方をあらわにしていると言えるでしょう。言い換えれば、中国は国内では強権的な統治を行う一方で、国内における報道は同時にまた他国の視線を意識しているわけです。

これら国内、国外に向けての相反する態度は常に政治的な「覆い隠し」の背後で機能しているのであり、これこそが中国という特異な政治的空間をもたらしているのではないでしょうか。すなわち中国という空間は「覆い隠されること」と「あらわにされること」との間で

延々と揺れ動き、事実とフィクションは国の境界の内外に住むどちらの人々にとっても容易に区別され得ないのです。

引用文献　Bibliography

序論　**Introduction**

Anderson, J. (2010) *Understanding Cultural Geography: Places and Traces*. London and New York: Routledge.

Carruthers, M. (1990) *The Book of Memory: A Study of Memory in Medieval Culture*. Cambridge, Melbourne and New York: Cambridge University Press.

Cosgrove, D. and Jackson, P. (1987) "New directions in cultural geography", *Area*, 19(2), 95-101.

Cresswell, T. (2004) *Place: a short introduction*. Oxford: Blackwell Press.

Driver, F. (2013). Imaginative geographies. In P. Cloke, P. Crang, and M. Goodwin (Eds.), *Introducing Human Geographies*. London and New York: Routledge, pp. 234-248).

Engelland, C. (2020) *Phenomenology*. Massachusetts and London: MIT Press.

Farley, P and Symmons Roberts, M. (2012) *Edgelands: Journeys into England's true wilderness*. London: Vintage.

Fox, J., Morosanu, L., and Szilassy, E. (2012) "The Racialization of the New European Migration to the UK", *Sociology*, 46(4), 680-695.

Gillborn, D. (2010) "The White Working Class, Racism and Respectability: Victims, Degenerates and Interest-convergence", *British Journal of Educational Studies*, 58(1), pp. 3-25.

Heidegger, M. (2003) *Being and Time*. 23rd edition. Oxford: Blackwell Publishing.

Jackson, P. (1989) *Maps of Meaning*. London: Routledge.

Kundnani, A (2001) "In a foreign land: the new popular racism", *Race and Class*, 43(2), 41-60.

Lynn, N., & Lea, S. (2003) "'A Phantom Menace and the New Apartheid': The Social Construction of Asylum-Seekers in the United Kingdom", *Discourse and Society*, 14(4), 425–452.

Malpas, J. (2008) *Heidegger's Topology: Being, Place, World*. Cambridge, Massachusetts and London: MIT Press.

Massey, D. (2005) *For Space*. London: Sage.

Mitchell, D. (2005) "Landscape" In Sibley, D., Jackson, P., Atkinson, D. and Washbourne, N. (Eds.) *Cultural Geography: A Critical Dictionary of Key Concepts*. London and New York: I.B. Tauris, pp. 49-55.

Poole, E. (2011) "Change and Continuity in the Representation of British Muslims Before and

After 9/11: The UK Context", *Global Media Journal: Canadian Edition*, 4(2), 49–62.

Seamon, D. and Mugerauer, R. (1985) "Dwelling, place and environment: An introduction" in Seamon, D. and Mugerauer, R (Eds.) *Dwelling, place and environment: towards a phenomenology of person and world*. Dordrecht, Boston, and Lancaster: Martinus Nijhoff Publishers, pp. 1–14.

Thurgill, J. (2014) *Enchanted geographies: Experiences of place in contemporary British landscape mysticism*, unpublished thesis manuscript, last modified November 2014.

Thurgill, J. (2019) "Un/Mapping Sacrality in Kamakura: Towards a (meaningful) spiritual cartography", *Living Maps Review*, No. 6, pp. 1–9.

Viala-Gaudefroy, J. and Lindaman, D. (2020) "Donald Trump's 'Chinese virus': the politics of naming", *The Conversation, Wednesday*, April 22 2020. Online at: https://theconversation. com/donald-trumps-chinese-virus-the-politics-of-naming-136796

Watsuji, T. (1935) *Fūdo (trans. Climate and Culture)*. Tokyo: Iwanami Shoten.

Wood, V. (2020) "Daily Mail takes title of UK's most read paper from The Sun after 42-year run", *The Independent*, Saturday 20 June. Online at: https://www.independent.co.uk/news/ media/daily-mail-the-sun-circulation-most-read-newspaper-uk-a9576761.html

① 赤門　#1 Akamon

Heidegger, M. (2000) *Introduction to Metaphysics*. Yale: Yale University Press.

Cresswell, T. (2004) *Place: A Short Introduction*. Oxford: Blackwell Press.

Turner, V. (1969) *Ritual Process: Structure and Anti-Structure*. London: Routledge and Keegan Paul.

② 三四郎池　#2 Sanshiro Pond

Heidegger, M. (1971) *Poetry, Language, Thought*. New York and London: Harper and Row.

Mitchell, D. (2000) *Cultural Geography: A Critical Introduction*. Oxford and Malden: Blackwell.

③ 1号館　#3 Building I

Harman, G. (2011) *The Quadruple Object*. Hampshire: Zero Books.

④ 総合図書館　#4 General Library

Ingold, T. (2007) *Lines.: A Brief History*. London: Routledge.

Till, K. (2005) *The New Berlin: Memory, Politics, Place.* Minneapolis: University of Minnesota Press.

⑤ 駒場池　**#5 Komaba Pond**

Kant, I. (1998). *Critique of Pure Reason.* Cambridge: Cambridge University Press.

Cresswell, T. (2004). *Place: A Short Introduction.* Oxford: Blackwell Publishing.

Heidegger, M. (2003) *Being and Time.* 23rd Edition. Oxford: Blackwell Publishing.

⑥ 数理科学研究科棟　**#6 Mathematics Building**

Norberg-Shulz, C. (1980) *Genius Loci: Towards a Phenomenology of Architecture.* New York: Rizzoli Press.

⑦ オンライン教室　**#7 Online Classes**

Derrida, J. (1982). *Margins Of Philosophy.* Chicago: University of Chicago Press.

Plato. (2008). *Protagoras.* Cambridge: Cambridge University Press.

⑧ オンライン空間　**#8 Online Space**

Agamben, G. (1998). *Homo Sacer: Sovereign Power and Bare Life*. Stanford: Stanford University Press.

Agamben, G. (2000). *Means without end: Notes on politics*. Minnesota: University of Minnesota Press.

謝　辞

何よりもまず、連載記事と本書の制作に精力的に取り組んでくれた円光門氏に深く感謝する。本連載に対する彼の揺るぎない献身がなければ、この本は実現しなかっただろう。非母語で取材を行い、それを書き起こして邦訳するというのは、多くの人にとって大変な作業だと思うが、彼はこの本の制作に必要な作業量にも動じることなく、大学生活の文化的、歴史的、政治的な地理学についての書物という、東大生をはじめとする学生にとって価値のあるものを制作してくれた。

記事を毎月読み、コメントし、発表することを承認してくださった東京大学教養学部英語部会のアルヴィ宮本なほこ教授と小林宜子教授、過去2年間に行われた取材に関するさまざまな許可をくださった東京大学広報の古瀧はるか氏には心から感謝する。毎月記事を掲載し、本書の出版を支援していただいた東京大学新聞、このプロジェクトを実現してくださったシーズ・プランニングの長谷川一英氏にも謹んで御礼を申し上げたい。

105

また、このプロジェクトの初期段階で貴重なアドバイスと励ましをいただいた東京大学のシーラ・ホーンズ教授、板津木綿子教授、矢口祐人教授にも感謝する。常にサポートしてくれた英語部会の同僚や、知識に対する貪欲さで私を驚かせてくれた学生たちにも御礼したい。

私の家族と妻のカットには永遠の感謝を捧げる。彼ら彼女らの揺るぎないサポートと励ましがなければ、私は自分の夢を追いかけ、アカデミアでキャリアを積むことはできなかっただろう。

毎月の記事を読んでくださる熱心な読者の方々や、この本で初めて私たちの記事を知ってくださる方々がいなければ、このプロジェクトはそもそも存在し得ない。本書が皆さんに、人文地理学という現在進行形のプロジェクトへの新たな熱意をもたらし、自己を取り巻く場や空間に驚きを見出すことを願ってやまない。

ジェームズ・サーギル

本研究はJSPS科研費 20K12954 の助成を受けたものです。

106

本書は、東京大学新聞の連載記事「サーギル博士と歩く東大キャンパス」を加筆・修正したものである。

大学2年の春、連載記事の企画書を手に、駒場Iキャンパスにあるジェームズ・サーギル博士の研究室を訪問したことが、ついこの間のように思い返される。それからおおよそ月に一度のペースで、博士とともにキャンパスのさまざまな場を訪れ、そこで取材を行い、和文と英文の記事を東京大学新聞に発表してきた。博士からは、取材内容に関することだけでなく、私の稚拙な英文についても多くのご指導をいただいた。何よりもまず、サーギル博士に深い感謝を申し上げたい。

本書の元となった連載記事もまた、多くの東京大学新聞編集部員の方々のご協力なしには実現し得なかった。なかでも、企画書の初稿をチェックして適切な助言をくださった武沙佑美さん（教養学部卒）、真っ先に面白そうな企画だと背中を押してくださった高橋祐貴さん（文学部4年）、記事のチェッカーとして私の文章表現や論理展開などに多くの重要なアドバイスをくださった衛藤健さん（総合文化研究科修士1年）と山中亮太さん（文学部4年）、の

みなさんには特に感謝を申し上げたい。また、第五章のハイデガー哲学に関する記述にあたっては、宮田晃碩さん（東京大学総合文化研究科・博士後期課程）にご協力いただいた。

書籍化に際しても同様に、多くの方々のご理解・ご協力をいただいた。編集部員の小田泰成さん（学際情報学府修士1年）は、書籍化に対する私の熱意を汲み取ってシーズ・プランニングの長谷川一英さんに繋いでくださった。市橋紅呂瑛さん（教養学部4年）は、本書の冒頭に収めたサーギル博士による論考の和訳についてご協力をお願いしたところ、快く引き受けてくださった。東京大学本部広報課と総合文化研究科・教養学部事務部総務課広報・情報企画チームの方々には、東大キャンパスの画像を本書に掲載する許可をいただいた。東京大学新聞常務理事の村瀬拓男さんは、書籍化に必要な経費などについて直ちにご承認をくださった。謹んで御礼を申し上げたい。

最後に、本書がこうして無事に形となったのは、シーズ・プランニングの長谷川一英さんのご尽力によるものである。本当にありがとうございました。

円光門

東京大学のキャンパスの中でも、最も象徴的な場所が安田講堂だろう。内田祥三が設計したこの講堂は、1925年に竣工して以来、日本においては大学の学術的優位性を表象するものとされてきた。

我々は本来であれば、安田講堂における空間体験を考察する記事をもって本プロジェクトを終了する予定であったが、新型コロナウイルスの蔓延によりキャンパスが閉鎖されたため、キャンパス内での調査、取材ができなくなってしまった。しかし、この不在の構造こそが、我々と同じように東大の数地内に入ることができなかった学生の空間体験を描き出すことを可能にする。実際、本書の中で、そしておそらく多くの新入生の心の中で、安田講堂は東大キャンパスの中心における空白の役割を果たしており、感染拡大以降東大にやってきた多くの人々の経験の中で、注目すべき不在の空間となっている。

まさに、安田講堂を本書から外すことは大きな意味を持つ。安田講堂は、それ自体が象徴的な建物であるだけでなく、我々が持つ東大のイメージの中心でもあるからだ。だが安田講堂は、この「幽霊的」――一時的ではあるが――な存在として我々の生活の中で捉えられているにもかかわらず、現在も過去も含め、学生や教職員の地理的なイメージの中にしっかりと固定されている。だからこそ我々は、この不在を受け入れ、他の文章では言及されていないこの講堂の写真を本書の中央部に載せることにした。とはいえ、ともすれば不在を通じて存在するしかない安田講堂をここに載せるという決定は、一つの問いを――我々がこの本で行った考察を通じてその答えを見つけようとした問いを――含んでいる。すなわち、不在が存在の内に含まれるとはどういうことか？

安田講堂

A Todai Philosophical Walk
with Dr. Thurgill
Toward a Geographical Interpretation of Place

James Thurgill & Mon Madomitsu

Production Assistance : The Todai Shimbun

サーギル博士と巡る東大哲学散歩
—場の地理学的解釈に向けて—

発行日	2021 年12月28日 第1刷発行
著 者	ジェームズ・サーギル／円光 門
編集協力	公益財団法人 東京大学新聞社
発行者	長谷川一英
発 行	株式会社 シーズ・プランニング
	〒101-0065　東京都千代田区西神田 2-3-5　千栄ビル 2F
	電話 03-6380-8260
発 売	株式会社 星雲社（共同出版社・流通責任出版社）
	〒112-0005　東京都文京区水道 1-3-30
	電話 03-3868-3275

©James Thurgill, Mon Madomitsu 2021
ISBN978-4-434-29925-4　Printed in Japan

【執筆者紹介／About the Authors】

ジェームズ・サーギル(James Thurgill)

2014年にロンドン大学ロイヤル・ホロウェイ校卒業、Ph.D.(文化地理学)を取得。英ノーサンプトン大学、ブルックランズ・カレッジ、ロンドン芸術大学の助教を経て、2017年より東京大学教養学部特任准教授。伝承、情動、空間経験に関する文化的、文学的地理学を研究テーマとし、国際的な査読付きジャーナルや論集にて幅広く著作を発表する。現在はJSPS科研費の助成を受けた「Literary Geographies of Folklore」(2020-2023年)の研究代表者、およびウェールズ大学出版会から近刊予定の『文学的地理学──理論と実践』シリーズ編者を務めている。

Dr. James Thurgill graduated from Royal Holloway, University of London, in 2014 with a Ph.D. in Cultural Geography. After serving as an assistant professor at the University of Northampton, Brooklands College, and University of the Arts London, UK, since 2017 he has been project associate professor in the College of Arts and Sciences at The University of Tokyo. His research is primarily concerned with the cultural and literary geography of folklore, affect, and the spatial experience, and he has published extensively on these themes in international, peer-reviewed journals and edited volumes. Dr. Thurgill is Principal Investigator of the four-year JSPS-funded "Literary Geographies of Folklore" (2020-2023) and co-editor of the newly established *Literary Geography: Theory and Practice* book series by University of Wales Press.

円光　門（まどみつ・もん）

東京大学法学部第3類（政治コース）4年。東京大学新聞編集部員。ピアニストの角野隼斗、園田涼、作曲家の野村誠、美学者の小田部胤久をゲストに招いたシンポジウム「音楽に神は必要か」（東京大学駒場キャンパス、2019年）を主催、国際会議「東京フォーラム2020」に学生スピーカーとして参加。2022年度より東京大学大学院法学政治学研究科総合法政専攻修士課程進学予定。

Mon Madomitsu is a senior in political science at the Faculty of Law, The University of Tokyo. He serves as a member of the editorial staff for the university newspaper, Todai Shimbun. In 2019, Mon organised "Does Music Need God?" a symposium featuring pianists Hayato Sumino and Ryo Sonoda, composer Makoto Nomura, and aesthetician Professor Tanehisa Otabe, held at Komaba Campus, The University of Tokyo. Mon was selected as a student speaker for the Tokyo Forum 2020 international conference. From 2022, Mon will be studying at the Graduate Schools for Law and Politics at The University of Tokyo.

Table of Contents

Fig.1, Fig.2　©Yuki Takahashi
Fig.3–Fig.18　©Mon Madomitsu

Envisioning Worlds: on the importance of geographic thinking

James Thurgill

Objective

This book is something of an experiment, a set of spatial interrogations designed to introduce readers to two of The University of Tokyo[Todai]'s iconic campus spaces, Hongo and Komaba I, via a geographic interpreration. The purpose of this is twofold: firstly, to present the various buildings and spaces belonging to the university, which many readers of this book will no doubt be familiar with, via a set of cultural geographic analyses and theoretical provocations that should reveal those overlooked and marginal elements of space that all too often go ignored. Here, I refer specifically to the history of the campuses, their architectural forms, the demarcation and organisation of the campus spaces, the movement of individuals who use or pass through the campuses, and various other geographical features of the sites.

Secondly, and more broadly, the collection of interviews gathered here works to highlight the ways in which places – even "ordinary" places such as universities – are produced through a layering of time, memory, and imagination, and encountered

in innumerable ways by the individuals who pass through them for reasons of work, study, leisure, and so on. We are generally unaware of the underlying factors that configure the physical (material), emotional and sensorial (immaterial) makeup of such places and the experiences we have in them. To this end, we hope that readers of this book will herein find new ways to see, imagine, and experience the places they encounter in their daily lives. Moreover, it is hoped that readers of this book can go on to apply the ideas presented in this collection to their own analyses of the places and spaces they occupy, that it will prompt *you* to think "geographically" about the world you live in, to uncover the social, cultural and historical traces and presences that work to form the places people live, work, and play.

Origins

This volume is comprised of interviews taken from "Take a Walk through Todai's Campuses with Dr Thurgill", a monthly serial article published over a two-year period (2019-2021) in the *Todai Shimbun*, The University of Tokyo's student newspaper. Credit for the publication of these articles goes to Mon Madomitsu, who not only came up with the idea for the article series but who painstakingly transcribed and translated each of the interviews presented

in this book, working to condense the many hours of discussion from our meetings into succinct and engaging readings. While the core idea of the articles was to apply the theory and methodologies of cultural geography to an examination of space, our discussions and analyses spanned the work of architecture, history, literature, philosophy, and politics, and numerous other cognate disciplines. To this end, the conceptual basis of this work is truly interdisciplinary and not limited to a single reading or methodology, which we hope will appeal to a wide range of readers of different backgrounds and interests.

Another important point to note here is that readers will identify a clear change in trajectory in the latter half of the book, where we deal with the conceptualisation and experience of online spaces, that is to say: virtual geographies. While many of the interviews took place in person and on campus, the outbreak and rapid spread of the novel coronavirus COVID-19 made it impossible to conduct the interviews safely in campus spaces. Given the project's focus on actual-world, physical sites, the closing of the university's campuses and the necessary restrictions on movement and interaction led us to rethink our approach and the ways in which *place* and *space* might be discussed here. It quickly became necessary for universities across the world to redefine

classroom spaces, not in terms of their physical dimensions, lighting, arrangement of seating and so forth, but in terms of what exactly qualifies a space of learning, how this might be achieved within a virtual setting, and how students and staff would experience the "new normal" of learning and working remotely. From a cultural geographer's perspective, the rapid implementation of online teaching in the early months of 2020, a rethinking of how we successfully utilise and experience space in a meaningful way, and the technological developments necessary for creating a valuable learning experience online, are all of great interest, and useful for considering what we mean when we talk about geography. Thus, readers will note that a number of the essays that appear in this collection are aimed specifically at addressing issues of distance, presence, and absence in online environments and discuss the implications they may have for us in the physical world. The articles that follow this introductory essay revolve around a thematic core of memory, narrative, place, and mobility, all of which remain central to decoding the various spatial forms that cultural geographers are interested in. These conceptual strands are interwoven throughout the interviews, offering readers an insight into some of the key themes of cultural geographic enquiry.

Trajectory

As previously mentioned, this collection of interview-based essays attempts to analyse the places and spaces of two of The University of Tokyo's most well-known campuses, Hongo and Komaba I, and some of their key features, through the lens of cultural geography. For many readers, the term "geography" will likely be interpreted as meaning physical geography; the study of the morphology of the natural landscape, its mountains, deserts, rivers, arable lands and so on, which exist as part of our surrounding environments. For others, the word geography may be thought of as the mapping and surveying of terrain, tracking population growth, demographic transition, and geopolitical borders. It could even be that geography prompts images of municipal planning, of rural and urban division, of place names, trade routes, territories and conflicts. In truth, geography is all of these things and much more.

While there is certainly a distinction to be made between physical geography (the study of landforms) and human geography (the study of people and places), geography itself is intimately bound up with the existence of all things. That is to say, geography relates to *everything*, therefore *everything* can be

considered from a geographical perspective. This is not to say that geography is a discipline without precision or focus; to the contrary, geography is a discipline that studies the multitude of spatial relationships – proximity, distance, movement, interaction, transgression – that exist between particular things and the specific spatial contexts that these relationships produce. When geographers say that *everything* is *geography*, it is not a baseless claim or a sweeping generalisation about the supposed importance of the subject; the point is rather more about the way that all things exist as objects set both in time and in space. It is the spatial dimension that geographers are particularly interested in and it is on this that they focus their enquiries.

The word geography derives from the ancient Greek *geographia*, which simply means "Earth writing" or "Earth description". In its purest form, then, geography is a way of describing the world we live in; it is the study of places, spaces and the relationships between people and their environments, both lived and imagined. Thus, geographers investigate both the material properties of the Earth and the human societies and cultures that are distributed across its surface. Of course, not all geographers are interested in the same aspects of geography and several subdivisions exist within the

discipline (cultural geography, historical geography, literary geography, political geography and so on).

Time and Space

Cultural geography, a subfield of human geography from which this book draws many of its core ideas and methodologies, is the study of the places, spaces, and landscapes where culture is produced. The geographer Jon Anderson states that "culture" describes all aspects of human activity, and that geography – *where* things happen – is what gives context to this activity (2010). This suggests, then, that the things we do in our daily lives gain specific meaning(s) from the places and spaces where we do them. We often think about historical events in this way, imagining that certain happenings, ideas, conflicts etc., occurred as they did specifically because of the time in which they unfolded. For example, the common misconception that people once believed the Earth was flat is regularly used to provide context for historical understandings of world geography, i.e., that people held a specific belief or vision of the world at a specific time from which we have now progressed. By doing this, we clearly show that historical moments are given (or at least imagined as gaining) context as a result of the time in which they occurred, whether that be down to scientific or technological

limitation, societal structure, or religious belief is of no concern. The point is that time, and more commonly history, is considered to be the determining factor in understanding why things happen the way they do.

But, of course, time is only one of the dimensions in which all things operate. Geographers focus on the way(s) that space, too, provides context for ideas, politics, beliefs, customs, happenings, and all the other things that take place to shape our daily lives (both now and in the past). In her seminal 2005 work *For Space*, geographer Doreen Massey highlights the importance of this dimension, demonstrating how space is the product of ongoing interrelations – from the molecular to the global –, and that, despite attempts to define it otherwise, space remains heterogenous, multiple, and always in the process of production (p.9). Various approaches have been taken to try and better understand this spatial dimension and how it affects our being-in-the-world. The Japanese thinker Watsuji Tetsurō, for example, focused his philosophical enquiry *Fūdo* (1935) on the intimate relationship between climate and culture, and moreover, the importance of recognising spatiality as a key aspect to existence. Watsuji's work on climate was itself something of a critique of German philosopher Martin Heidegger's preoccupation with

time. Along with the writings of key Western figures such as Nietzsche and Kierkegaard, Heidegger's work was particularly important to Watsuji's own philosophical development and *Fūdo* functions as both an homage to and criticism of the German thinker's work. Despite the marginal attention given to place by Heidegger in his own ontological analysis, the role of space and place – that is to say, of geography – in Heidegger's writings has acted as a continuous source of inspiration for geographers and philosophers alike. Heidegger's notion of dwelling, in particular, has prompted a number of enquiries into the transgressive nature of place: "[d]welling incorporates environments and places but extends beyond them, signifying our inescapable immersion in the present world as well as the possibility of reaching beyond to new places, experiences and ideas" (Seamon and Mugerauer, 1985, p. 8).

No discussion of Heidegger and spatiality would be complete without the mention of Australian philosopher, Jeff Malpas. Throughout his career, Malpas has worked to survey Heideggerian spatiality; a spatiality that is, in essence, premised upon Heidegger's conjecture that all things exist within an ever-growing topology, one that can only be measured by a being's closeness or connectedness to the world around it (Malpas, 2008, p. 76). Malpas insists on

the significance of place in Heidegger's ontology and elucidates the role of *dwelling*, a process that is both temporal and spatial in nature, as a conduit through which to understand the agency of both humans and non-humans in relation to each other (Malpas, 2008). As Tim Cresswell comments, for Heidegger, "(p)lace as dwelling, then, is a spiritual and philosophical endeavour that unites the human and natural worlds" (2004, p. 22). As will no doubt become obvious as you read through the interviews that follow, Heidegger's writings have been hugely influential on my work as a geographer, largely on account of the spatial ambiguity that his philosophy affords us.

For Heidegger, the world is a site of exposure and concealment: things – people, objects, tools, – are always in a state of revealing themselves to us, yet we are only ever able to view part of that which we observe, just one aspect at a time (2003). This is a development of what Heidegger's mentor, Edmund Husserl, described as *adumbrations* in his phenomenological work, the "many shadows a thing itself casts as it is explored by us" (Engelland 2020). To this end, Heidegger presents a geography replete with adumbrations: absent-presences and present-absences, a world of things that are never fully within our grasp. This interpretation of spatial perception is useful in that it helps us to understand

our experience of place as occulted, always partially obscured by the present form. In the discussions that follow, I implement this thinking as a way to elucidate the manner in which places reveal themselves to us through the traces, fragments, and memories of their now near-hidden aspects. This requires playing the role of a sort of "place detective" on the hunt for historical and geographic clues to the stories behind the development of Todai's campuses and our connections to them.

Place

At the root of geographic enquiry is place, the thing that allows us to form attachments to specific sites and find meaning in the experiences we have there. Place, more than any other concept in geography, I would argue, is at the core of how we fix ourselves to the world. Place is not only imagined but also memorised – our memories, like our bodies, are subject to the same two dimensions as all other things: the temporal and the spatial. The twelfth-century theologian Albertus Magnus claimed that it is inconceivable to recall anything in our minds without first fixing that memory to a place (Carruthers, 1990). *How exactly would one go about locating an ageographic memory?* If all experiences take place as both a *where* and a *when*, how, then, can the spatial

element be detached from the temporal element that is being recalled? Even our earliest memories not only detail the people and emotions we experienced, but the places (either accurately or inaccurately recalled) where they happened. Thus, when I think of my grandfather, who died when I was a teenager, I picture him in the very places in which I encountered him in life – his favourite chair, his tool shed, my grandparents' garden. He is not recalled as an amorphous figure, a colour, or sound without spatial context, but is instead fixed and located within a collection of remembered geographies.

As humans, we think in places. As animals, we think in places. We might suppose this to be true of all animals capable of complex thought processes; of those who migrate to remembered places; those who hibernate, hidden away in locations only they can recall; of those that travel to breed in specific destinations year after year; and of those that habitually seek prey in particular hunting grounds known only to them. Our world, like theirs, unfolds before us as a multiplicity of retained placial experiences, each one hidden away somewhere deep within the recesses of the mind. All of these places become stored, recalled and recollected as we occupy and inhabit the multiple and complex spaces around us. One could logically conceive, then, that not all

places are new to us, but rather, spatial experiences are at least in part the result of a multitude of existing memories, layered and stratified, piled high and unknowingly brought to consciousness; a standing reserve that we perpetually borrow from in order to make sense of our surroundings (adapted from Thurgill 2014, pp. 85-86).

Imaginative Geographies

A key tenet of cultural geography is the understanding that the places, spaces, and landscapes we live in and move through are themselves formed through social relations (Mitchell 2005). By this we mean to say that, while an external physical terrain exists around us – a physical geography of earth, rock, water and air, – it does not exist independently of human action. As historical geographer Felix Driver has noted, geography is something that not only exists in tangible forms such as fields, mountains, rivers, etc., but is imagined, represented, and shaped by our own thinking and by that of those around us (2013). Driver uses the term "imaginative geographies" to describe how our ideas about the world are formed through processes of abstraction, exoticisation, and alienation. Taking the example of nineteenth-century British maps (and their makers) to illustrate the power and influence of imperial thinking on the

geographic imagination, Driver demonstrates how people's understanding of geography can be distorted and their perceptions of national identity, social development, and cultural value manipulated in order to implement (otherwise unjustifiable) social and racial hierarchy.

Maps are an interesting place to begin when discussing the ways in which geography is imagined differently in different places by different people. For example, if you're reading this book in Japan, then you will no doubt be familiar with world maps that situate Japan at their centre – Japan is fixed as the central point from which the outside world emerges and from which all things revolve. Compare this with a world map produced in the UK, for example, and you will find Great Britain occupying that same central position, replacing Japan at the centre of the world, its culture and its economy. In this sense, geography is not only about the ways we connect with the world on a physical level but equally concerns how we imagine the world to be and how these imaginings are represented. An important point to note, then, is that "imaginations are social as well as individual" (Driver 2013) and as such the geographical imagination, including that represented in and by maps, is of a shared nature. It is through this collective process of representing and imagining others that we come

to view people from different villages, towns, cities, regions, and countries not as the individuals they are but as stereotypes based on where they live, where we live, and how we've seen them represented.

Even on national and regional scales, maps and mapping are often produced with the same prejudice. As Paul Farley and Michael Symmons Roberts write, maps are always created through a process of abstraction (2012). Maps are never objective: they have been carefully considered, with decisions made on what should and should not be included within them. As visual representations of the landscapes we live in, maps are integral to the way we think about and navigate the world around us. The prejudices of the cartographer thus become our own. Mapping is just as much concerned with what remains absent, left off the map, as it is a record of what is actually there. As I have argued elsewhere, to this end maps can be repurposed as tools for creativity. By exploring those places that have been undermined, unrepresented, and unmapped in official cartographies it becomes possible to "make meaningful experiences of place that allow for a deeper and more nuanced understanding of our surroundings" (Thurgill 2019, p. 9).

Representational Geographies

Representation gained the attention of human geographers in the late twentieth century, who found it a useful conceptual framework for showing how geographies are imagined and interpreted differently according to social processes, overarching political structures and ideological systems (e.g., capitalism, communism, imperialism, nationalism, racism, etc.) (Anderson 2010). Influenced by the work of post-structuralist thinkers such as Roland Barthes and Michel Foucault, and the semiotics of Ferdinand de Saussure, these representational cultural geographies were used to examine how people's understandings of the world are produced and to demonstrate how these understandings gain meaning through shared systems of signs and cultural coding that exist on specific local, regional, and national levels (See: Cosgrove and Jackson 1987; Jackson 1989). While contemporary approaches to cultural geography tend to focus on the non-representational and more-than-representational ways in which geographies emerge, are experienced, lived, and performed, the value of representation for geographic analysis should not be overlooked.

The geographical imagination – the way we think about and visualise the world around us – is not only shaped by mapmakers, of course, but more

commonly through the representations offered to us by literature, cinema, television, advertising, politics, and news broadcasting, or rather through the words and images delivered to us by authors, directors, politicians, and media corporations. We only need to look at national newspapers to see the ways in which our perception of geography and geographic boundaries can be manipulated. Flicking through the pages of one of the more politically conservative newsprints in any country can quickly reveal the way that imagined borders are created and physical borders reinforced. The UK's *Daily Mail*, for example, has a long-standing history of publishing stories that portray immigrants, minority ethnic populations, the LGBTQ+ community, and their political rivals, in a particularly negative light, and has received much criticism from scholars as a result (See: Kundnani 2001; Gillborn 2010; Fox et al 2012). Given the *Daily Mail's* rise to become the UK's most-read newspaper (Wood 2020), the affective nature of its printed political bias and ongoing misrepresentation should not be ignored. The real-world effect of such journalism has been to shape the way that readers think about people of a different geographic origin, ethnicity, political stance, sexuality, or religion to themselves in increasingly negative ways, often through stories alluding to violence, terrorism, and

other forms of anti-social behaviour. Here, geography is used to create a spatial Other. This Othering is produced via a narrative that insists on individuals of different racial, ethnic, and cultural backgrounds to that of the host country being intrinsically rooted in outside geographical locations, incompatible with people outside of their own cultures, and thus presenting the perceived "foreigner" as an existential threat (Lynn and Lea 2003; Poole 2011).

National, regional, and local borders are continually reinforced in our minds through this kind of (mis) representation. Political rhetoric and media bias regularly go hand-in-hand in defining the way people think about geography and their relationships to different geographic areas, distorting the public's vision of the world and its peoples. A timely example of this can be seen in the language used by former President of the United States, Donald Trump, in his televised addresses on COVID-19. The intention behind the former president's words has not been overlooked by political commentators, who noted "The deliberateness of the wording was made clear when a photographer captured the script of his speech wherein Trump had crossed out the word "Corona" and replaced it with 'Chinese'" (Viala-Gaudefroy and Lindaman 2020). Trump's labelling of the virus as "Chinese", "Wuhan Flu" and "Kung flu" set a

very specific spatial parameter for the source of the infection, namely China.

Such language has come to affect the way that people think about China in broader terms, not only with regard to the virus but more generally as the antagonist of Western democracy. As a result of the loaded (geo)political rhetoric surrounding the new coronavirus, it is China and the Chinese people who have become imagined as the real threat in the minds of many living in the West. A torrent of conspiracy theories aimed at "exposing" China's supposed culpability continues to flood online forums, often with little or no intervention from administrators. While "Stop Asian Hate" currently trends on Twitter, we need only look to Trump's anti-Chinese rhetoric as having sown the seeds for the anti-Asian sentiment now sweeping the USA, and which recently culminated in the murder of six women of Asian origin in an Atlanta spa. This is not to say that Trump himself is responsible for the killings – he is certainly not the only political figure to have flirted with racist and xenophobic language since the outbreak of the virus – but it is a crushing reminder that words have consequences, and when you use words to victimise and stigmatise people of a particular ethnic origin, when you purposefully play fast and loose with the truth in order to perpetuate

geopolitical rivalry, and when you knowingly conflate infection with ethnicity, then you may as well be the person pulling the trigger.

Why Geography Matters

Of course, these kinds of representational geographies are not the only sort to affect the way we imagine the world around us. Literature, art, music, film, and theatre are all equally responsible for forming the geographic imagination. The worlds that unfold from books, television, and cinema screens, the landscapes depicted in poetry, painting, and dance, each add another impression to the maps we create in our minds. While it is important to remain critical of the ways in which geographies are represented, we must also consider the vistas afforded us through the imagination of others, whereby we get to see the world through a different lens. Such a process is just as worthy of academic scrutiny; for stories, movies, manga, and pop songs each play a part in creating a new image of the world. How the media, artworks, songs, video games, books and so on that we consume shape and determine our understanding of other places, both actual and fictional (and which are often drastically different to our own), is hugely significant to understanding the geographical imagination. Moreover, to echo Jon Anderson's claim that place

provides the context for culture (2010), we can assess the role of cultural depictions of geographies not only in terms of what they represent but also by who and where they are being represented.

Geography is not only important for understanding how culture represents, but more importantly where those representations are formed. Depictions of Tokyo on screen, for example, can tell us about the way the city is viewed based on where the film is made and who its intended audience is. We can see that the geographic origin of a cultural text, such as a documentary, is important for understanding representation, deciphering meaning, and assessing the way a particular place is imagined simply by looking at the criticism that text receives from a native audience. For example, Western depictions of Tokyo often focus on the hypermodern and futuristic elements of the city; the chaos, neon lights, and ever-crowded streets, continuing a representation of Japan as exotic, mysterious and otherworldly that was initiated in the nineteenth century. When Tokyo features in Japanese cinema, however, it often forms a far more neutral city setting; a mundane backdrop in which people live, work and play. This does not merely express an East/West divide, such disparities in representation exist in all parts of the world and on national, regional, and local levels.

But certainly, such differences highlight gaps in the perception, experience, and imagination of those doing the representing and those places that are being represented.

Geography is, then, far more complex than might first appear. Cultural geographers navigate past, present, and future imaginings of places, spaces and landscapes, and they understand geographies as being produced through human interactions, attachments, and activities of all varieties. But most importantly, cultural geographers emphasise the reciprocal relationship between people and place, highlighting the various ways in which places are produced by people and people produced by places, both physically and in the imagination.

#1 Akamon, Hongo Campus

Absence Recognized Through Presence

"Why are there beings at all instead of nothing?" This is a question posed by the philosopher Martin Heidegger, who regarded what we do not see as "absence". Dr. Thurgill pays attention to "spatial absence" at the entrance of Akamon as an interesting point to consider the space around the famous gate. Unlike other gates in the Todai campus, Akamon is roofed and is surrounded by a thick wall (Fig 1). As such, when we stand in front of Akamon and look into the Todai campus, we cannot see the world beyond, which is veiled by the gate's frame and wall, and so it appears to be absent to us. The action of going through the gate, however, allows the world beyond to unfold before us, and thus absence turns to presence.

"Absence is recognized through presence, and vice versa," says Dr. Thurgill. In other words, by grasping the space that is veiled by Akamon and which thus appears "absent," we come to understand that the landscape of the Todai campus, as it is perceived through the gate, is but a part of the whole. Such an understanding of "spatial absence" invites us to see what is still unseeable, to imagine what lies beyond the gate.

Dr. Thurgill points out that the Akamon embraces such a paradox, inviting people to enter while simultaneously regulating their movement and vision. Cultural geographer Tim Cresswell has suggested that a disturbance to people's mobility, such as traffic congestion or airport departure gates, is a type of "friction". According to Dr. Thurgill, the Akamon also produces friction by regulating the movement of people who pass through it (Fig.1).

(Fig.1) Akamon produces "absence", and also adds "friction" to the movement of people.

Akamon has one large door and two small doors (see above), and according to the door that is open, people's view of and movement in the space will differ. It is only through the gate (the framework) that people can view the landscape beyond and

move towards it. Heidegger used the word "Gestell"-enframing-to explain that the way of being is prescribed by environment. The structure of Akamon is indeed Gestell, which regulates and prescribes the movement of people's physicality.

In addition, Dr. Thurgill employs the concept of "liminality", proposed by the anthropologist Victor Turner. This concept points to a transgressive change, and Turner regarded places such as shrines or churches, where people enter and experience a transformation that makes them move away from their daily life, as "liminal places". Dr. Thurgill, however, thinks that the university is also a liminal place, for people there retreat from the mundane world and engage in academic life. Akamon indeed functions as a boundary line between two such places.

Between two different regions, there exists some sort of a wall, if not a physical one then one that is imagined. In order to get access to another region, we need a gate. Nevertheless, we should be careful when following the path through it. By composing "spatial absence", the gate certainly has a function that invites people into it, yet through nothing but the composed "absence" it engenders, it produces friction on people's movement.

In today's globalizing society, it is not difficult to think of a "different culture" as an example of a "wall"

which is close to us. Such a wall may be physical, as the former US President Trump proposes, or imagined, existing only in one's mind.

Generally speaking, placing not a wall but a gate between different cultures is the first step toward interaction. If we take "cross-cultural exchange" too flippantly, however, might we not end up spreading the belief that those we interact with are no more than people who entertain us by providing us with an extraordinary "liminal place"? Or might we not end up producing friction among those who are about to move through the gate, consequently emphasizing the wall more than what is beyond it? In case of the interaction among different individuals, what should we suppose beyond the framework of wall and gate? Such questions are worth contemplating while enjoying the view of Akamon.

#2 Sanshiro Pond, Hongo Campus

A Struggle Between the Man-made and the Natural Worlds

As can be seen in water pollution or global warming, we humans commit acts of "violence" against nature through environmental destruction. Dr. Thurgill points out that Sanshiro Pond offers us an opportunity to reflect upon such an exploitative relationship between humankind and nature by highlighting the tension that exists between humans and the natural world. We can find demonstrations of nature's tenacity and resistance to human control all around us, even on a small scale. The rocks positioned around the pond, for instance, are uneven and slippery, making its visitors' foothold unstable and revealing a side of nature that cannot be controlled by humans (Fig.2).

In addition, the perceived 'closeness' between human beings and nature that is felt at Sanshiro is worth mentioning. "With the picturesque nature of Sanshiro Pond before us, we begin to perceive nature not as something we utilize, but instead come to respect the agency of nature itself and feel affection toward it."

"Is this, however, 'real' nature?" questions Dr.

Thurgill. "The geographer Don Mitchell proposed a critical-geographical view of landscape, which at a first glance seems to be natural yet, in fact, is nothing but a 'representation' made by human hands." Similarly, the nature of Sanshiro Pond gives us the impression that it has existed from ancient times, that it is somehow organic. Nevertheless, typical

(Fig.2) "I feel relaxed in this beautiful natural environment," was a phrase we heard several times when conducting our interviews at Sanshiro Pond.

"natural" elements, such as plants, trees, rocks, a waterfall, the fish and terrapins living in the pond, and the cries of birds, are in fact artificially curated and managed as if the scene were in a museum.

More surprising is that such a representation urges us to construct a non-violent relationship with nature, yet the place itself has actually been

composed through the very violence we seek to avoid. In other words, to maintain the beautiful environment of Sanshiro Pond, to execute periodic care such as replacing the water in the pond or removing the weeds in and around it, all mean to some degree that we commit violence against nature. "All forms of 'maintenance' apply a certain level of 'violence'," states Dr. Thurgill. Yet, the water in the pond gets murky and the weeds still flourish; this is because nature is reclaiming what was taken away by human beings.

This relationship between the man-made and the natural at Sanshiro Pond is reflected in the following argument of the philosopher Martin Heidegger. In his "The Origin of the Work of Art", Heidegger posits that a work of art is born from a tension between "World (Welt)" and "Earth (Erde)". The "World" unfolded by an artwork attempts to cut away from the "Earth" – namely the physical components of the work itself, its raw materials and so on, which together operate to provide the work with context and give meaning to the "World"– yet the "Earth", in turn, attempts to veil the "World" and hide its meaning.

How, then, can we apply this argument to Sanshiro Pond? Sanshiro Pond, or the "work", is born from a tension between the artificially represented 'nature', or the "World", and its physical components, namely the

'real' nature, or the "Earth" (water, land, trees, etc.). But nature is, of course, only a representation here, a reference to an idealized natural environment, and has been composed and maintained through a physical cutting away of the Earth, through an enacting of violence against nature. Nature, on the contrary, attempts to reclaim that which was stolen by human hands, through "veiling" or hiding itself within the curated representation. As such, behind the precious beauty of Sanshiro Pond is a relentless struggle between the man-made and the natural worlds.

Does it follow, then, that the affection we feel toward nature at Sanshiro Pond is meaningless? Is the reflection upon violence, which is itself realized through violence, completely futile? Dr. Thurgill denies such a view: "We ought to be conscious of the contradictions the status quo contains, yet simultaneously we ought to accept its beneficial points. This is what it means to 'think critically'." We are not to praise the 'natural' beauty of Sanshiro Pond flippantly, nor are we to feel hopeless about the violence that realizes its beauty. Rather, we need to recognize the violent background on the one hand, but embrace the affection toward nature that Sanshiro Pond offers us on the other; such an attitude can lead us to a better understanding of environmental protection.

#3 Building 1, Komaba Campus

The Past Haunts This Place

"History can be discovered through a kind of 'everyday archaeology'. Material traces of the past surround us in our daily lives, just waiting to be uncovered, but they frequently go unnoticed" says Dr. Thurgill. Building 1 is indeed a place well suited to discovering such 'traces' (Fig.3). Above an archway leading to the courtyard remains the crest of the former Ichikou, First Higher School of Tokyo (Fig.4). In the same place, beneath our feet, lies a manhole cover where another of Ichikou's emblems can be found embossed within its metal surface. Looking through the corridor windows inside the building we can catch a glimpse of a staircase, possibly leading down to the rumoured underground tunnels, which are said to have been constructed as a safety precaution for disasters, air raids, and so on, but which are now sealed off and inaccessible.

Building 1 was constructed in July 1933, ten years after the Great Kanto Earthquake. With its looming clock tower and Gothic-style architecture, a rarity on Komaba campus, the building gives an anachronistic atmosphere to its surroundings. Extraordinary narratives rooted in the history of Building 1, such as

that of the former High School students who are said to have climbed the clock tower in order to surveil the skies for bombers during the Second World War, or the underground tunnels believed to run beneath the building (which some students say continue as far as Shibuya), are undoubtedly born from the uncanniness of Building 1 and have been handed down through generations of Todai students.

But what is the origin of this uncanniness? According to Dr. Thurgill, it is due to the fluctuation of the temporal axis caused by the present being affected by past materials. "The past, though at the present being regarded as absent, is made manifest by materials that signify traces of history, and which continue to linger in the present. As if it were a ghost that is not

(Fig.3) The overgrown plants are at both edges of Building 1

supposed to be there, the past haunts this place."

The uncanniness of Building 1 can be perceived not only temporally but also spatially. Due to the overgrown plants at both edges of the building and a large tree in front of the main entrance, we can never observe the whole building at once, not even from a distance, unlike the Yasuda Auditorium in Hongo. Moreover, we cannot go through the courtyard enclosed within the building (Fig.4). In order to move to the opposite side of the main gate we must orbit around Building 1, for the gateway to the courtyard, primarily designed as a place of relaxation and which might otherwise allow for free movement within the centre of the building, is closed off by an iron fence. We cannot identify the building as a whole; neither

(Fig.4) The closed-off courtyard and the crest of the former Ichikou, the First Higher School of Tokyo.

can we gain access to the centre of it. We may be left with the impression that the 'essence' of Building 1 is always somewhat veiled and elusive.

Inside the building, this elusiveness grows even stronger. On entering the structure we arrive at dark, narrow corridors and wherever we stand, we can only see one of the four sides of the building. In other words, there is a constant shifting of our view as we turn the corner and are once again prevented from seeing the building in its entirety.

Both the past signified through material traces and the restricted view framed by the organisation of the building share a commonality of concealing and revealing time and space respectively, as Dr. Thurgill points out, "something is always veiled in our experience of the world". The past is veiled as an absence; we can touch it only through the material traces that remain. It is the same with Building 1, a space that does not permit us to grasp the whole structure at any one time. To be sure, every single being is vacillating in-between complete presence and complete absence, just as the philosopher Graham Harman writes, "Objects are units that both display and conceal a multitude of traits."

#4 General Library, Hongo Campus

History as a Curation of Traces

"'History' is a curation of traces, and 'place' can be thought of as sites where these traces pile up." The relationship between "history" and "trace" which Dr. Thurgill describes is represented prominently in the space surrounding the General Library.

The General Library (Fig.5) was built in 1928 after the original library, which opened in 1877 with the founding of The University of Tokyo, was destroyed by fire in the wake of the Great Kanto Earthquake. Since its opening, the General Library has undergone several periods of repair and

(Fig.5) The construction of the underground section of the General Library began in 2015

renovation. In 1986, Prof. Sachio Otani from the Faculty of Engineering took charge of the renovation of the library square and set mandala mosaics into the ground there to express mourning for his former Todai classmates who had died in the Second World War.

However, due to the construction of the underground section of the library that began in 2015, the mandala mosaics were removed and have never been replaced. Instead, the foundations of the original library along with a collection of stones that once formed a water channel for the Kaga Family were discovered during the renovation process and have taken the place of the commemorative mandala. The former was processed and reused to form benches around the

(Fig.6) The foundations of the original library were shaped into the benches

(Fig.7) The water channel for the Kaga Family

fountain (Fig.6), while the surfaces of the latter were cut off and set into the plaza's surface, positioned just as they would have been during the Edo Era (Fig.7).

As such, within the space around the General Library there exist multiple traces from different ages; but while some traces are conserved, others are removed. Ultimately, the curation of these traces comes to form and represent the "historical narratives" of the place now occupied by the General Library.

The Edo period water channel, the library's original Meiji Era foundations and the mandala stones that once acted as a material memory of the war: why were the former two conserved but the latter removed? According to Dr. Thurgill, some might hold

the notion that the reason for managing this area's spatio-historical narrative in such a way arises from a sense of "legitimacy", urging us to question whether or not the trace is historically rooted in the place. "The water channel and the foundation of the original library were originally there, physically in this place, but the mandala were placed there somewhat arbitrarily at a later stage. In this sense, perhaps the mandala stones were not viewed as 'legitimate' in the conservation process of the site," says Dr. Thurgill.

However, Dr. Thurgill points out that such an argument regarding "legitimacy" is short-sighted: "Be it the water channel, the foundation, or the mandala stones, they were all arbitrarily created by human hands at some point. The only difference is that each is either older or newer than the other, relatively speaking."

Another reason that can be considered in the removal of the mandala stones is that there might be an active attempt to depoliticize and neutralize the library square by removing the memory concerned with the war, which, after all, is an extremely political and contested topic. Dr. Thurgill maintains, "It may be thought that this square, where the neighbors take their dogs for a walk, families have pleasant talks, and students discuss their academic topics, futures, and such, is not an appropriate place

for political features to be displayed."

However, is there such a place that could not be considered political? Every trace is related to a time or space that no longer exists: thus, a trace is nothing but a kind of memory. The water channel and the foundations of the original library are, in other words, material memories. The Irish geographer Karen Till maintains that a memorial place is created within the interplay between "performances" and "politics". A memory can be preserved in a public space both because there are "performances" in which people regularly go there and remember an event, and because there are "politics" in which a certain authority determines which memory is accurate, legitimate, and appropriate for future conservation. In the determination of memory, there functions a power-balance among authorities with various agendas: "Therefore, even the water channel and the foundation of the original library, which at first glance appear to be unrelated to politics, politicize the library square simply through their being positioned there."

The act of depoliticizing is itself a political action. "The mandala stones were originally designed purely as a memorial to the war dead," says Dr. Thurgill. "In spite of this, it might have been judged that the image of war, which is often associated with empire

and exclusionism, is not appropriate in the place of the university, a place which is supposed to be inclusive and progressive." Nevertheless, in the end, such a judgement can be nothing but political.

Memory of the War Retained in the Space

Has the memory of the war, then, been completely erased from the university's landscape? According to Dr. Thurgill, such a view is negated.

Firstly, so far we have perceived the library square as layers of traces from various ages, and we have pondered which layer appears as the strongest, and which the weakest. Yet the library square represents these traces not only vertically in terms of their being framed within a hierarchy of perceived historical significance, but also horizontally, sitting alongside each other as constituent parts of the present.

It is well-known that the General Library was built in the "Uchida Gothic" style, named after its architect, Uchida Yoshikazu. Dr. Thurgill points out that there appears to be an element of the Art Deco included within this unique Gothic style. "If we take a closer look at the shapes created by the roof or the framing and positioning of the windows, we come to realize that there are clear Art Deco influences in the design: we can observe the repetitive patterns

(Fig.8) The mixture of Gothic and Art Deco

and emphasis on linearity that are characteristic of the Art Deco style" (Fig.8). In other words, Gothic, an architectural style of the European Middle Ages, and Art Deco, which emerged in the early twentieth century, appear to coexist side-by-side, without either one overshadowing the other.

Moreover, the General Library consists of one large building along with four other additional institutions. Of these four institutions, the Historiographical Institute, built in 1928 was the first to be constructed. That same year, the General Library was built; while the Centre of Media (which later became the Graduate School of Interdisciplinary Informatics), the Centre of Sociology, and the Faculty of Education were built in 1953, 1954, and 1955,

respectively. The old and new tiles adorning the building are different colours and belong to different historical periods from before and after the Second World War, each coexisting side-by-side on the outer wall of the same building. Therefore, as we reinterpret the library square within a context not of "vertical layers" but of "horizontal coexistence," the memory of the War whose layer was once removed, is obliged to return to the place where various ages coexist.

Secondly, places are, according to Dr. Thurgill, palimpsestic. A palimpsest is an old document upon which already-written words have been erased and new ones written. While the once-erased words cannot always be detected clearly with the naked eye, their traces remain, providing ghostly suggestions of the former text. Places can offer us the same insight into their past, if we look for the traces of history that remain within them.

The British anthropologist Tim Ingold states that traces exist in two forms – additive and reductive. In other words, a trace can be a marker either of presence or absence. There should be no doubt that the water channel and the foundation of the original library, by being set in the very place we now find them, function as traces that signify the past of the site. Yet we also need to regard the mandala, which

was removed from the square, as an obvious trace as well. The memory of the war still remains here, it lingers, barely perceptible.

◇

According to Prof. Naoyuki Kinoshita (Cultural Resources Studies), the mandala originally refers to a design scheme of the whole library square by Prof. Otani, and thus its trace continues to be present in spite of the loss of the mosaics themselves. The foreground handrail in Fig.9, for example, was designed by Prof. Otani, while the handrails along the other three sides were newly designed by Prof. Kawazoe, who is in charge of the present renovation; as such, the former can be regarded as a "trace" of Prof. Otani's legacy.

Why did Todai not make more of an effort to

(Fig.9) There were once mosaics under this handrail

retain the memory of the war? To that question Prof. Kinoshita answers, "Because Todai had negated everything concerning the war at the time of the defeat of Japan." There was once an investigation within Todai that sheds light upon "the Departure of Students for the Front", at the fiftieth anniversary of Japan's defeat, yet the target of the investigation was limited to examining "the Departure of Students for the Front", and no attempt was made to go beyond and verify the role played in the Russo-Japanese War and so on. Prof. Kinoshita remarks, "'Oblivion' – this is the right word for us."

#5 Komaba Pond, Komaba Campus

Meanings Found in a Superstition

"I know it exists, but I've never actually been there." Perhaps a number of Todai students would answer in such a way when being asked about the Komaba Pond (so-called "Ichiniro-Pond"). Indeed, while I walked around the pond for more than an hour with Dr. Thurgill in order to conduct the interview for this article, not a single person visited the place.

It is well known that students of the university do not always have a positive impression of Komaba Pond. This is evident in campus folklore, which claims that applicants to The University of Tokyo will fail their entrance exam if they visit the pond. It is also said that current students of the university could be equally affected, running the risk of having their graduation delayed by a year or two as a result of the pond's legendary "curse". In his cultural geography courses for freshmen and sophomores, Dr. Thurgill often gives the students an assignment requiring them to write horror stories on atmospheric spots within the campus grounds. Subsequently, many students choose the Komaba Pond as the setting for their stories, focusing on the eerie impression they

have of the place to create an ominous backdrop for their tale. For instance, in their work for the class students often describe the story of a ghostly hand stretching from the pond, reaching for a nearby student in an attempt to drown him or her.

Why has the Komaba Pond become a place of such uncanniness? One reason might be that much of the area remains unknown to us: the "off-limits" area is much larger than the accessible space, and several chain barriers are positioned around the pond in order to emphasize the restriction of access (Fig.10). Yet, the motivation behind our entry being prohibited is concealed, resulting in an unearthly atmosphere which permeates the site. The trees growing along the promenade that surrounds the pond hinder us from

(Fig.10) Chain barriers that emphasize the restriction of access

(Fig.11) The trees along the promenade hinder us from gaining a panoramic view of the area

gaining a panoramic view of the area (Fig.11), as if to further enhance this uncanniness. Indeed, it appears that we are not allowed to have a full understanding of this place.

"An ordinary explanation may conclude that the site's visitors, by perceiving the secluded geographical situation of the pond, could feel some kind of uncanniness there, and that such an experience may have shaped the strange folklore regarding the failure of the entrance exam or the graduation delay," says Dr. Thurgill. "Yet, I believe that it is also possible for the process to occur the other way around." In other words, there is a possibility that a visitor's perceptual experience is shaped by the folklores or

their preconceptions regarding a certain place.

Let us now contemplate how the superstition of ghosts influences people. Dr. Thurgill questions, "Even those who profess not to believe in ghosts often admit to being afraid of spending the night somewhere associated with them, like in a graveyard, for example. But if they think it is neither possible to see nor feel ghosts, then what exactly are they afraid of?" In order to solve this problem, we might posit that people are more concerned with the "association" between the object (in this case the graveyard) and the superstition surrounding it (the ghost), than they are with the object itself.

Why is the role of "association", then, so strong? In one of his major works, *Critique of Pure Reason,* the philosopher Immanuel Kant maintains that to acquire a meaning is to connect a concept with an object. Concept is that which is thought up within one's mind, while object refers to something external, that which exists outside of the body. Kant regards thinking prior to experience as being "empty", and that taking in the information of the outside world without considering what it might mean as "blind". Kant suggests that it is only by connecting concept and object that meaning can arise.

As such, the reason why people posit there to be more importance on the "association" between an

object and a superstition rather than on the physical properties of the object itself is that they wish to find a meaning there for themselves. When the "concept" of uncanniness that emerges from the strange folklore concerning Komaba Pond is connected with "object", i.e. the secluded geographical situation of the pond itself, our perceptual experience conjures up a meaning. This is also the moment in which Komaba Pond is born as a "place", for as the cultural geographer Tim Cresswell states, "When humans invest meaning in a portion of space and then become attached to it in some way it becomes a place."

The World That Unfolds on Each Occasion

In the previous section, we have shown that "space", when its meaning is invested through human attachment, turns into "place". From this perspective, it can be thought that Komaba Pond, as a space, is a single, homogenous area, yet understood as a place, we might perceive it as divided into at least two parts.

As discussed above, within Komaba Pond there exist both "off-limits" and accessible areas. In the accessible area, one can actually walk to the very edge of the pond, thus it is possible to perceive that area as a "place" through the physical and emotional attachments we can forge there.

The "off-limits" area, on the contrary, allows

us to be involved in the space only through our looking down into the area from the higher ground surrounding the pond from which the steps lead down, or through our reading of the map at the entrance to the pond. "Looking down" is not a good option here, for there are overgrown trees surrounding the site that work to obscure our view. In order to grasp the whole area we must depend upon the map alone to provide us with a complete view of the site. Yet a physical experience like that we can enjoy in the accessible area is impossible from glancing at a map, as Dr. Thurgill states, "A map is nothing but what is abstracted and idealized from a space." Consequently, the two areas – the accessible and the "off-limits" – exist differently as places.

This point becomes even more apparent when considered through the German philosopher Martin Heidegger's concept of "world". According to one of Heidegger's major works, *Being and Time*, the world is not simply given to us as a preexisting geometric space; instead the world unfolds before us every time we encounter things that surround us. The world becomes known to us through our being-in-place.

As an example, let us consider the bridge that crosses both edges of the pond. This bridge is not a straight line, but has a change in angle at its center, as if it were composed of two rectangular plates that

had been slid and conjoined side-by-side (Fig.12).
Due to the short width and the lack of a barrier along
the edges of the bridge, we must initially focus our
attention on the placement of our feet so as not to lose
our footing as we walk across the bridge. What we
heed in this moment is actually our movement over
the water, and upon this relationship between the
water and our bodies, an understanding of the world
– and our being within it – begins to unfold. (If you
are lucky enough, at this point you may even witness
a snake swimming vigorously from one side of the
pond to the other, as I did during this interview).

Gradually, we get used to the bridge and our
focus shifts to the landscape on the right side of the
pond. This is because to the left exists a less well-
maintained area of the pond, consisting mostly of

(Fig.12) The bridge that crosses the pond

(Fig.13) The end of the pond

rocks and weeds (Fig.13). Whereas on the right, there unfolds an unobstructed view of the pond's surface, surrounded by well-shaped trees. Here unfolds another new world for us to perceive.

Yet as we reach the midpoint of the bridge, both our view and our body are somewhat forced toward the left, coerced into following the direction in which the path of the bridge is turned. Consequently, we will now encounter the world that is the end of the pond.

From the Heideggerian concept of "world", it can thus be understood that each time we physically engage with the diverse phenomena in the accessible area of Komaba Pond, the world appears to us differently, and consequently we encounter the

diversity of "place". Contrastingly, such an encounter with "place" is impossible in the "off-limits" area, whose location we can confirm only by looking down from the high ground or from checking the map.

Dr. Thurgill points out that our perception of the end of the pond will eventually lead to the perception of the whole pond. Since Komaba Pond is long and narrow with a curve in its middle, if we stand on the bridge and look toward the right, it seems as if the pond were an endlessly flowing, continuous river. Yet by looking at the "end" of the pond to our left, we can finally understand that this is not a river that flows far ahead of us, but is instead a pond with clear limits and a fixed locality. Dr. Thurgill thus states: "Just as we come to understand the pond itself through perceiving the end of its waters, presence only becomes perceivable to us when it is preceded by absence."

#6 The Mathematics Building, Komaba Campus

Organicity Behind Inorganicity

The Mathematics Building (Fig.14), which stands at the edge of Komaba campus, is often referred to by students as the "Mathematics Hospital". The bare concrete appearance of the building and the blunt look of the entrance hall (Fig.15) might perhaps contribute to giving us the impression of a hospital-like structure. Together with the stereotypical view of students majoring in mathematics as "unfashionable", we might feel the building is somewhat unappealing. Yet, the truth is, those who call this building "hospital" do not look at the entire building so

(Fig.14) The Mathematics Building on Komaba Campus

(Fig.15) Blunt look of the entrance hall

carefully as to see how it functions as a space. "Speaking from the perspective of cultural geography, I think this building is one of the most successful buildings on the Todai campus," says Dr. Thurgill.

Some may wonder as to how a cultural geographer can speak properly about buildings. How successful buildings are in terms of their feeling or function as a structural form is, perhaps, a matter best left to the architects who design them. Dr. Thurgill states, however, that "thinking about how buildings fit into, affect and create spaces is also a geographical matter."

Once we step into the Mathematics Building, we can immediately see that, beyond our expectation, it does not have a purely utilitarian structure, neither

is it focused solely on the efficiency of people's movement as a "hospital" might be. Constructed to fit into the sloped ground of this area, the building has a section where the border between the first floor and the basement level becomes ambiguous (Fig.16). Another interesting feature worth noting is the auditorium, which is itself an independent structure that has been built partially inside and partially outside the main building. As such, its labyrinth-like structure of corridors, gallery areas and mezzanine floors urges us to gain a multifaceted understanding of its space. Thus, there is a certain fluidity of the space found in the Mathematics Building that we might not initally expect to find. Additionally, the repetitive geometric shapes of triangles and squares that are spread throughout the interior of

(Fig.16) Corridor that has a complex structure

the building seem to portray the lively essence of mathematics itself, as opposed to our first impression of this building as something blunt and rigid.

Now let us pay attention to the Yanaihara Park which unfolds in front of the Mathematics Building (Fig.17). "This building has a strong connection not only with mathematics but also with the surrounding area," says Dr. Thurgill. Compared to the bright, glass-walled Komaba Library which stands beyond the park, the Mathematics Building has a less welcoming atmosphere. The circular-shaped Yanaihara Park that lies between these two structures, however, subtly binds the spaces together: the softening afforded by its "roundness" seems to harmonize the surrounding materials. In this way, the Mathematics Building maintains its connection to

(Fig.17) Yanaihara Park

other places on Komaba campus.

Dr. Thurgill points out, "The use of green and brown on the outside of the building, which at first looks somewhat inorganic, actually resonates with the colours of the trees and the sands in Yanaihara Park." The building blends in and coexists with its surroundings as if it were a part of nature. Just as the architectural theorist Norberg-Schulz maintains that building deciphers a human understanding of nature into built form, the Mathematics Building, by integrating itself into its surroundings, works to reveal our understanding of nature.

From where, then, comes the idea that the Mathematics Building's features appear inorganic and dull? At a first glance, the whole building looks like a flat wall, thus making us think of a border that marks the limit of the campus – this may have accentuated the impression that the building is located on the very edge of the campus where there is no sign of human activity. Yet, in the moment when we become mindful of the windows above us that are set at a specific angle (Fig.18) , and which invite the reflection of the sunlight upon them, the building that reflects the sky, which is itself borderless, is no longer just a wall; it turns itself into a being that transcends the border.

There will be a change in our initial impression

(Fig.18) Windows that reflect the sky

of this building if we begin to think in such a way. For as we come to perceive the building as a part of nature, it ceases to be merely an inorganic block of concrete and instead becomes a place that we would like to explore.

A Todai Philosophical Walk with Dr. Thurgill

#7 Online Classes

[Part 1]   Do Online Classes Lack Place?

The 'places' which we have so far investigated have all been physical sites. However, the outbreak of COVID-19 led to all Todai campuses being closed in an effort to prevent the spread of infection. The only access to Todai available to us during this period has been through online classes. While the situation may yet improve, at the time of writing this book, access to the university remains restricted, and students continue to engage in online learning for many of their classes. However, can an online class be considered a place that is a target of cultural geography?

"Much work has been done by cultural geographers to examine the role of 'place' in the virtual world," says Dr. Thurgill. According to cultural geographers, a 'place' is a site in which human beings fix 'meaning' through the connections they make there. "'Meaning' comes from what a 'place' evokes in us, such as emotional responses and memories."

As such, an online class can be called a 'place' in so much as we are able to cultivate memories through interaction with teachers and students, and thus find our own meaning there (Fig.19). "A 'place' is imagined

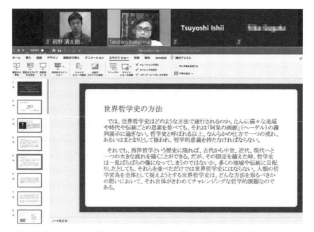

(Fig.19) A scene from a lecture offered by the East Asian Academy of New Liberal Arts. Zoom is used to elicit the students' active comments.

as if it would exist in real space, but regardless of whether it be real or virtual, the process of place-making is always one that begins in our minds."

What kind of meaning and experience, then, can we acquire in an online class? Dr. Thurgill unfolds his argument by utilizing a Heideggerian term "veiling" – a process through which the being of a thing is concealed. "In an online class, the participants' bodies and faces are concealed if the camera is off, and their real names are veiled if their display names are manipulated. Indeed, online classes allow for a type of 'veiling' to occur that would not be possible in the

physical classroom setting."

According to Dr. Thurgill, such "veiling" embraces two conflicting meanings. Firstly, the individual's loss of corporeal presence in online spaces makes the generation of spontaneous interaction among participants difficult. Where we might ordinarily react to expressions, gestures, and see the free flowing of ideas, the anonymity of online presence does not always permit such interaction. Yet at the same time, the veiling of that which shows individuality, such as faces or names, appears to reiterate a sense of unity among students: "There is a sense of unity knowing that everybody, while struggling with the same inconvenient situation, is learning from behind a computer screen. Paradoxically, this necessary 'absence' of students in the physical classroom provides them with a shared understanding of each other's 'presence' in the virtual one. That is to say, the now universal experience of being kept apart, 'hidden away', so to speak, can also work to bring us closer together."

"Does our very treatment of these two types of geography as oppositional – real versus virtual – not represent our over-dependence on physical, external environments?" questions Dr. Thurgill. "We have assumed and privileged the physical presence of 'actors' in the field of communication, which is to say,

the sense that 'one is actually there' has been based solely upon being tangibly present. But I think such a 'hidden' fundamentality of our everyday thinking is being gradually deconstructed in the practice of online learning. We are moving towards a different understanding of what it means to be 'present' in our everyday lives."

The things that surround us in the physical world, including languages, pictures, music, and even facial expressions, are all types of sign, in so far as they represent certain meanings. According to the French philosopher Jacque Derrida, a sign is what represents the deferred presence of that which it signifies. Things in our everyday physical world seem to be there in front of us, but in reality it is the opposite: those things in front of us are, in many cases, no more than mediations of presence(s), signs that signify meanings – substitutions for the thing itself. For example, that someone is standing right in front of me does not mean that I am immediately apprehending his or her being. The facial expression that represents emotions, the skin color that represents race, the language that conveys speech and transmits meaning – only by mediately going through these various signs can we begin to reach the being of that person.

Hence, it can be concluded that the difference between online and offline classes is not of a great

degree. In the online class, we cannot reach the beings of teachers and students other than through a multitude of signs displayed on our laptop screens. Such a structure of mediacy, however, is found in a physical classroom as well. Perhaps we should not stick to the dichotomy of real versus virtual anymore.

[Part 2]   Power and Space

In Part 1 of the chapter we have considered the online class from a perspective that focuses on 'signs'. However, there is another aspect that is yet to be considered; namely, how does the lack of physical sensation, which is often assumed to be a characteristic of the online world, affect our spatial perception? This question shall be explored in Part 2.

So far we explored the commonality between online and physical classes. This time, we contemplate the negative aspects of online classes based on their differences to physical space, and consider how we can overcome these issues through a transformation of our thought. Here we have two subjects of discussion: the loss of corporeality and the limit of mobility.

Firstly, it is clear that the absence of corporeality in online classes is one of the most important points to consider. Much of our communication happens nonverbally via body language. Most of the time, the nonverbal signals that we present in communication –

nodding, facial expressions, and so on – can easily be received by the person or people we are speaking to. For various reasons, online classes are restricted to audio only and there can be no perceivable nonverbal communication in situations where the web camera has been deactivated. The loss of corporeality in online classes means that there is a higher possibility of miscommunication occurring.

On this matter, Dr. Thurgill inquires: "Although it is undeniable that communication would be inadequate in such cases, might we not simultaneously find a positive side to the loss of corporeality?" According to Dr. Thurgill, such a positive could be the "democratization of place."

"Everyday we unconsciously encounter power relationships in the corporeal world," says Dr. Thurgill. That corporeality is, or that a (physical) body is in a space, means in other words that a body has a position. And the relationships of positions are frequently the relationships of power. "A boss sits at the head of the table during a meeting, a professor stands in front of a blackboard during a class while their students sit facing them. Each of these examples represents and maintains the actual power relationships at work." In online classes, however, an equally sized rectangular frame for each participant is displayed on a screen, regardless of whether the

user is a professor or a student. Furthermore, if we turn off the camera, there remains only one's voice and ideas. "As our experience of communication is "flattened" in online classes, we can say that the place where the class occurs becomes more democratic."

On the other hand, it should be noted that democracy is tied to the logic of exclusion. In his *Protagoras*, Plato, the father of Western political philosophy, posits that since God provides all humans with the virtue of justice, a democratic polity can only be attained if individuals collectively develop this virtue to become capable of deciding things through free discussion. This suggests, then, that all humans have a God-given right and responsibility to act and think justly. Yet, it is also remarked that God condemns those unable to actuate their virtues, regarding such individuals as harmful to democratic society and stating that they should thus be put to death.

As such, it is paradoxical that democracy, which is assumed to provide everyone with an equal footing, sometimes works in the direction of excluding those who cannot, for whatever reason, reach the same social or political ground as others. The situation is similar in online classes: online fora can only offer us an equal platform on which to learn if we assume a shared capacity to express "voice" and "ideas." This results in a person with no "voice" being at

greater risk of exclusion. Still, this problem is not an issue specific to online classes, but rather a problem internal to democracy and egalitarianism more generally.

So far we have paid attention to the point where the loss of corporeality weakens the power relationship. Yet on the other hand, we should not overlook the fact that the online system that creates such an environment can paradoxically work in the direction of strengthening the power relationship in favor of the host.

In Zoom, an online communication system that a number of universities currently use as their default online teaching platform, much of the power is concentrated on the host of a meeting room (which is, in most cases, a lecturer). A host has the power to mute participants' microphones and cameras, force them to move to another room, eject them from the meeting, and so on. Such an asymmetrical relationship between lecturer and student is not to be seen in physical classes. For a lecturer, no matter how much power he or she possesses, has no means but to depend on mere violence in order to take students out of the classroom or rob them of their voices.

Dr. Thurgill then answers to this problem as follows: "Places do not exist unless humans make them. This is the common understanding of place

shared by cultural geographers. It should not be forgotten, then, that the system of an online meeting room is nothing but a product of the Zoom company. It, too, forms a socially constructed place."

Should we take the framework of communication provided by Zoom for granted, the power relationship between a host and the other participants would be represented as something stable, the status quo. In order to deconstruct this power relationship, we should constantly question the very place that produces such a relationship in the first place.

Broadly speaking, the importance of acknowledging that a place is mediated by technology is not limited to the issues regarding online classes. "Nowadays, in the prevention of COVID-19 infection, there are more and more discussions as to the practical means to regulate human activities through the use of big data. In such a circumstance it is dangerous not to question the technology that shapes our daily life, and thus we must not take it for granted."

Let us now move on to the second subject of discussion, namely, the limit of mobility. This is a problem that bothers a number of university students, as we often see reflected in Twitter opinions claiming that taking online classes is like studying in a jail. Certainly, we university students can no longer simply go to a classroom by walking freely through our college

campuses. The only way to access online classes is to click the URL, and we cannot enjoy stopping by some place on the way from one classroom to another when we do so.

To this problem Dr. Thurgill questions, "Isn't the limit of mobility the same in our physical space?" The majority of a city consists of privately owned land, and we have no right to access most of the places that surround us. Even in a shop, there is a clear demarcation of the areas where customers have access to and those where they do not. Nevertheless, we feel as if there is a freedom of mobility in physical space. This feeling occurs only because we walk through a city by avoiding these inaccessible places without paying much attention to them.

"It is the demarcation of space that makes us notice the being of a place," says Dr. Thurgill. A place which has so far not been heeded well, presents itself in a radical way in online classes.

Yet, on the other hand, we might overlook one important factor – "time." The conclusion we arrive at on this occasion is one inferred from our focusing on "space." But if "time" is also something essential to mobility, how can we confront this problem? We would like to continue considering this issue with Dr. Thurgill in our next chapter.

#8 Online Space

Temporal Experience in Online Space

In the previous chapter, we have focused on the issue of how to overcome the disparity between physical classes and online classes. However, it became clear that we could manage to resolve such a disparity only to the extent that we had presupposed "space" as a fundamental factor in our experience. Indeed, we had overlooked another important dimension, "time". This chapter explores whether there is really an irreconcilable fissure between physical and online space.

"In order to say that 'time exists,' we should first of all presuppose space as a dimension fundamental to all existence," says Dr. Thurgill. Although Kant maintains that time is an inner intuition independent from space, we are, in fact, not able to experience such "pure time" without space. We usually perceive the passage of time based on events happening within a certain spatial context, in the form of "the sun has set," "my hair has grown long after not cutting it for a while," or "my back hurts after sitting for a long time". Time and space are closely interconnected in such a way, but how might the relationship between the two be experienced differently in physical and

online spaces?

As we have previously analyzed in the chapters discussing Komaba's Building 1 and Hongo's General Library, physical spaces contain layers of traces from various historic moments. This means that even if we stay in one place, we can sense the past, a depth of time, through the various things located there. Let us now call what signifies the movement between present and past the 'vertical temporal axis'. In contrary to this, let us imagine the movement from one place to another as the 'horizontal temporal axis'. The former refers to 'traces', while the latter describes 'mobility'.

According to Dr. Thurgill, the temporal experience in physical space always appears as a twofold process, consisting both of the 'vertical temporal axis' and the 'horizontal temporal axis'. As shown in Graph 1, the vector C can be derived from two axes, A and B. This means that as we move from one place to another, we may simultaneously trace back from the present to the past; for each step I take creates the possibility of encountering new traces in my surroundings, thus revealing the temporal "depth" of the site.

In online space, on the other hand, the situation is significantly different. We can say that the horizontal temporal axis remains intact, in so far as we can move from one 'place' – a website, for example – to

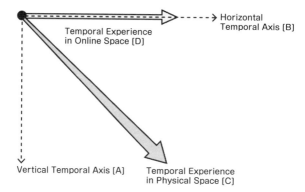

Horizontal
Temporal Axis [B]

Temporal Experience
in Online Space [D]

Vertical Temporal Axis [A]

Temporal Experience
in Physical Space [C]

(Graph 1) The difference between the temporal experiences of online and physical spaces can be explained by the vertical and horizontal temporal axes.

another. Yet, because there are no objects that might obviously display traces of the past, online space lacks any clear vertical temporal axis. Accordingly, vector D in Graph 1 signifies the temporal experience in online space, but since it does not have the same two-dimensional expanse as vector C, it becomes 'flattened'. Dr. Thurgill states that the difference in these temporal experiences is the decisive difference between physical and online spaces.

What meaning will the flattened, traceless temporal experience in online space bring to us? As even the archives, which serve as a place for the accumulation of memories, have become digitized, the "'now' will dissipate," says Dr. Thurgill. But what

does it mean for the 'now' to dissipate in the first place?

According to Dr. Thurgill, we are able to have the feeling of 'now' only insofar as we can relate ourselves to the archived past. "Just like presence only becomes perceivable to us when it is preceded by absence, the consciousness of 'now' only appears when placed in contrast to the past." Such a principle is true to the extent that the archives are ontologically limited in the way that they depend on certain media to give them form. For example, a gift from your departed lover is an archive that preserves the days spent with him or her, and an inscribed stone monument, for example, is a record preserving important events of the distant past. However, both a gift and a stone monument can only exist in the unique mediums we encounter them. In this way, the archive presents itself with an ontological 'vulnerability' in that the way it exists is extremely limited, emphasizing the fact that the event once existed but is no longer present, and as such emphasizing its contrast with the 'now'.

In online space, on the other hand, such a 'vulnerability' ceases to exist due to the digitalization of the archive. We can record online lectures and listen to them repeatedly; the same temporal constraints that effect any moment of physical space do not

appear to apply to the virtual world. Moreover, if we upload the data to a cloud system or transfer it to a USB drive, we can still watch the lectures on a smartphone even if our computer is broken, and on a tablet if our smartphone is broken. The specificity of time and space is distorted in this process. As such, the digitalized archive does not depend on specific types of media in the same way as physical records, thereby differentiating a relationship between 'an event that once existed' and the 'now' and eroding the temporal depth that we witness in the actual-world. In such a case, since an event in the past becomes repeatable, 'now' becomes ubiquitous. However, this virtual 'nowness' is different from the 'now' of offline or actual-world space. Dr. Thurgill calls such a phenomenon the "failure of 'now'".

Inclusive Exclusion and Exclusive Inclusion

As we have seen so far, physical space and online space embrace an unreconcilable fissure that stands between them with regard to temporal experience. But it is worth noting here that in all distinctions and boundaries, forces with opposite vectors are at work. The Italian philosopher Giorgio Agamben called such a field a 'threshold' (*soglia*).

A threshold is a place where two spheres simultaneously detach from and intermingle with each other. At

first glance, this process appears to be paradoxical, but Agamben's assertion is as follows; when one thing differentiates itself from another, it has to exclude the other from itself. Agamben discusses this through the example of politics and law, and is especially interested in the idea that states of exception ultimately reflect the status quo, rather than anything truly exceptional – that is to say that the exceptional is already included within the ordinary. There are two ways to execute this inclusion (Graph 2): 'inclusive exclusion,' in which one thing excludes another by including the latter within itself (such as an exception within the law that allows for the exceptional to be enacted without punitive action during a state of emergency), and "exclusive inclusion", in which a thing occupies an exclusive space within the sphere of the other, thereby excluding the other from within (for example, in the case of an occupied territory). Due to inclusive exclusion and exclusive inclusion, the boundary between two spheres of operation is simultaneously determined and yet blurred. Under such conditions, it becomes impossible to differentiate the exceptional from the norm.

Dr. Thurgill says that the concept of 'social distancing' shows the ambiguity of boundaries for similar reasons. Today's lifestyle, where we conduct classes or meetings

in online space and take social distancing measures in physical space, prompts us to be all the more conscious of the boundary between physical and online space. Dr. Thurgill points out that, "it feels somewhat paradoxical to see 'social', a word expressing 'nearness' among people, and 'distancing', a term that assumes some kind of separation, being forced together in a single phrase, because essentially we cannot be brought together if there is an enforced distance between us."

This implies that the moment physical space is differentiated from online space, then the distance experienced in the latter enters into the former as inclusive exclusion, or as exclusive inclusion when the nearness among people experienced in the former is brought into the latter. For instance, when we meet people in physical space (which necessitates being 'social'), we need to wear masks which means that we cannot see each other's face (which results in being socially 'distant'). Whereas, when we hold a meeting in an online space (which means, being physically 'distant'), of course we need not wear masks so can see each other's face and read their expressions (which is itself 'social'). Dr. Thurgill says, "We are simultaneously kept apart by being brought together, and are bought together, by being kept apart. Such a paradox is prompted by 'social distancing'."

As such, although there is a decisive boundary

between physical space and online space, that boundary is the very place where both spaces are differentiated from each other and yet simultaneously intermingle. In the age of 'With-Corona', we are constantly exposing ourselves to this boundary, and so the question is how might we best act to confront this conundrum? Are we to stick to physical meetings, suggesting that the times before the pandemic were better than they are today? Or are we to conduct everything online, concluding that the times have changed, and that distance is a necessary part of being social in today's society? Agamben maintains that if there is, at one place, one possibility that works against its opposing possibility, then "it is our task to use this possibility against it" (Agamben 2000:115). We can no longer interpret physical and online spaces in the traditional binary fashion. Instead, we are forced to face a shift in our perception of time and space in this new era.

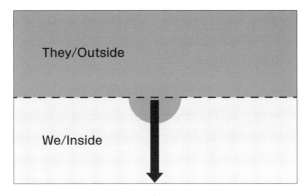

Graph 2-1

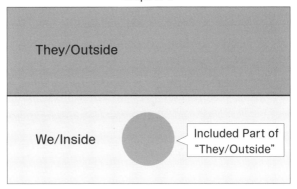

Graph 2-2

According to Agamben, any borders that might differentiate we/
inside from they/outside are not solid ones. In the process of
'inclusive exclusion,' because a part of they/outside is included
within the sphere of we/inside (Graph 2-1), the border between
we/inside and they/outside can be established by negating the
included part of they/outside (Graph 2-2).

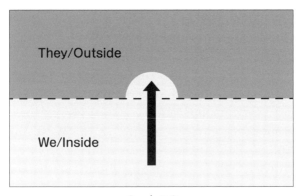

Graph 2-3

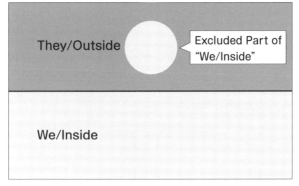

Graph 2-4

In the process of 'exclusive inclusion,' because a part of the we/inside becomes excluded in the sphere of the they/outside (Graph 2-3), the border between we/inside and they/outside can be established by negating the excluded part of the we/inside (Graph 2-4).

Special Interview:
Global Space Under COVID-19

—The spread of infection of COVID-19 does not remain solely the problem of medicine. It has also developed into a racial issue, where minorities, such as Asians in the West and Africans in China, have suffered physical attacks. What can you say about this from a geographical point of view?

"Culture" in cultural geography refers to all of the things that humans do, and human activities always unfold themselves within space. Cultural geography looks to understand how and why humans connect themselves to certain "points" in space and find meaning(s) there.

From a geographical perspective, xenophobic reactions attached to the pandemic might be analyzed in terms of how the "Other" has (re)appeared as people's spatial recognition changes. In the early stages of the pandemic, people all over the world, especially those in the West, thought that this was a "Chinese problem". For them, there was an imagined divide between China and the West.

—What happened after the Infection then spread to the West?

What is significant, here, is that the conflation of various Asian people living in the West to create a single, imagined "Asian Other" can be seen to have led to a new spatialising process. That is, people's perception of the infectious sphere as having a spatial limitation (i.e. China) has collapsed, while the presence of Asian individuals living in the West has made the threat appear geographically "closer" due to racial stereotyping and gross misunderstandings of the way viral contagions originate and spread.

–What can you say about things on the side of China from the geographical point of view?

There seem to be two distinct spatial spheres in which China might be seen to operate: [1] the economic sphere, where its capital and finance flow (relatively) freely to form a highly complex network of global trade routes and information connections, and [2] the more localized political sphere, where transmission of speech and information is suppressed. Both, perhaps, are symbolic of a contradiction that stands between China's outside perception as a global player and its internal national narrative that

dictates life *intra muros*. The alleged suppression of early reports on the coronavirus being made public is one of the many stories being picked up by global media in a backlash against China for failing to contain the virus in its early stages.

While the purported suppression of information and public discourse on the virus might look like a way for China to control its national narrative, it is, of course, not entirely separate from the state's move to regulate its international position as a major trader and manufacturer on the global market. Even if there appears to be a discontinuity between China's identity as a global player and China as an authoritarian political regime, the two are intrinsically linked.

To borrow an expression from Heidegger, the 'veiling' (Verborgenheit) of truth here – specifically the internal and external suppression of information regarding the pandemic – impacts on the way that China is perceived both within and exterior to its national borders. The 'controlling' of the Chinese press can clearly be seen as a method for limiting the economic impact of the pandemic that might otherwise occur through loss of its trading partners and/or halting the operation of its factories.

—Heidegger uses a pairing of the words 'veiling' (verbergen) and 'revealing' (entdecken) whose meanings are two sides of the same coin. Do you think such an ambiguity can be seen in China as well?

The 'veiling' process that takes place in the space between China's internal and external narratives seems to blur the distinction between the spatial spheres of China as an insular state and China as a global superpower, yet simultaneously it reveals the peculiar way of China's being. In other words, while China conducts tight governance inside the country, its press is acutely aware that the eyes of other countries are upon it.

These contradicting attitudes are, at all times, functioning behind a wall of political 'veiling', and this itself reveals a peculiar political space, whereby China oscillates in a perpetual state of 'veiling' and 'revealing', and where fact and fiction are not easily distinguishable for either those living within or outside of the country's walls.

Acknowledgements

First and foremost, I must express my deepest gratitude to Mon Madomitsu, who worked tirelessly in bringing the serial article and now this book into being. Without Mon and his unwavering dedication to the article series, this book would not have happened. Having to conduct interviews in a second language would be a daunting task for many people, not to mention transcribing and translating the information gathered, yet Mon remained unperturbed by the level of work involved in the production of this volume. As such, he has formed what I believe to be an invaluable series of works on the cultural, historical, and political geographies of university life both for students at Todai and those attending other institutions.

I would like to offer my most sincere thanks to Professor Nahoko Miyamoto Alvey and Professor Yoshiko Kobayashi of the Department of English Language at Komaba, who read, commented on, and approved each of the monthly articles published in the series. I also wish to express my heartfelt gratitude to Haruka Kotaki of the Public Relations Team at The University of Tokyo, for securing relevant permissions for each of the interviews held over the last two years. I am incredibly grateful to the

Todai Shimbun for publishing our monthly articles and for supporting the publication of this book, as well as to Mr. Kazuhide Hasegawa at Seeds Planning for his role in bringing this project to life.

A special thanks to professors Sheila Hones, Yuko Itatsu and Yujin Yaguchi of The University of Tokyo, who each offered invaluable advice and encouragement in the early days of this project. I also wish to thank my colleagues in the Department of English Language for their constant support, and my students, who never cease to amaze me with their voracious appetite for knowledge.

My family and my wife, Kät, have my eternal gratitude; without their unfaltering support and encouragement I would never have been able to follow my dreams and pursue a career in academia.

Of course, none of this would be possible without the dedicated readers, both those who engaged with our monthly articles and those discovering this collection for the first time with this book. Thank you for your support. I hope this collection brings you a new enthusiasm for the unfolding project that is human geography, and that you, too, come to find wonder in the places and spaces that surround you.

James Thurgill

This work was supported by JSPS KAKENHI Grant Number 20K12954.

This book is based on a revised version of a serial article in the *Todai Shimbun* entitled "Take a Walk Through Todai's Campuses with Dr. Thurgill".

In the spring semester of my second year at university, I visited Dr. James Thurgill's office on the Komaba I Campus with a proposal for the serial article. Since then, I have visited various places on Todai's campuses with Dr. Thurgill on an approximately monthly basis, conducting interviews and publishing articles in Japanese and English in the student newspaper. Dr. Thurgill has guided me extensively not only on the content of the interviews but also on my written English. First and foremost, I would like to express my deepest gratitude to Dr. Thurgill.

The series of articles on which this book is based would not have been possible without the help of *Todai Shimbun's* dedicated editorial staff. I would also like to sincerely thank Ms. Sayumi Take (graduate of the College of Arts and Sciences), who proofread the first draft of my proposal and offered me invaluable advice; Mr. Yuki Takahashi (Senior at the Faculty of Letters), who initially encouraged me to pursue this project; and Mr. Takeru Eto (2nd Year Master's student at the Graduate School of Arts and Sciences) and Mr. Ryota Yamanaka (Senior at the Faculty of Letters), who were proofreaders of the monthly articles and offered me many important

suggestions on the style and clarity of my writing. Mr. Akihiko Miyata (Ph. D. candidate at the Graduate School of Art and Sciences) kindly gave us advice on descriptions regarding Heideggerian philosophy.

I am also indebted to the many people who have helped with the publication of this book. Mr. Taisei Oda (1st Year Master's student at the Graduate School of Interdisciplinary Information Studies), a member of the editorial staff, understood my enthusiasm for the book and helped me contact Mr. Kazuhide Hasegawa of Seeds Planning. Ms. Chloe Ichihashi (Senior at the College of Arts and Sciences), who kindly agreed to help me translate Dr. Thurgill's essay included at the beginning of this book into Japanese. The Public Relations Office both at Hongo and Komaba campuses kindly gave permission to include images of Todai's campuses in this book. Mr. Takuo Murase, Managing Director of *Todai Shimbun*, gave his immediate approval for the expenses required for the publication of the book. I would like to express my sincere thanks to all of them.

Finally, it is the efforts of Mr. Kazuhide Hasegawa of Seeds Planning that brought this book into existence. Thank you very much.

Mon Madomitsu

Of all the places on The University of Tokyo's campuses, it is the Yasuda Auditorium that is the most symbolic. Designed by Yoshikazu Uchida, construction of the auditorium was completed in 1925, and is considered emblematic of the academic excellence the university is known for throughout Japan. We originally decided to conclude this project with an inquiry into the spatial experience of Yasuda Auditorium; however, due to the spread of Covid-19 the campuses were closed, and we were unable to conduct our research and interview on the campus grounds. As such, Yasuda Auditorium remains noticeably absent from our investigations. Yet, it is this very structure of absence that has allowed us to depict the spatial experience of all those Todai students who, like us, have been unable to gain access to the site. Indeed, in this collection, and perhaps in the minds of many of Todai's new students, Yasuda Auditorium serves as a lacuna at the centre of the university's campuses, a noted space of absence in the experience of many arriving at the university since the outbreak of COVID-19.

The omission of the Yasuda Auditorium from this collection of articles is obvious; it is not only an iconic building in its own right, but central to the image we have of the university. Despite this now, albeit temporary, 'ghostly' presence of the building

in our lives, Yasuda Auditorium remains firmly fixed in the geographic imaginations of Todai's students and faculty, both present and past. It is for this reason that we decided to embrace the absence afforded us and to place a photo of the Auditorium, which has not been mentioned elsewhere in our articles, at the centrefold of this book. Nevertheless, this decision to feature the otherwise absent-present Yasuda Auditorium here entails a question, one whose answer we have attempted to find through the investigations presented in this book: what does it mean for absence to be included in presence?

Yasuda Auditorium